The Children's Author

How to write picture books, short stories, chapter books and YA

Judy Lawn

The Children's Author

© 2018 Judy Lawn

ISBN – 13: 978-1726043151

www.judylawn.com
www.goodbounceback.com

Cover Design by Gabrielle Schollum
www.pinpointdesign.co.nz

This book is sold subject to the condition that it shall not, by way of trade or otherwise, be lent, resold, hired out, or otherwise circulated without the publisher's prior consent in any form of binding or cover other than that in which it is published and without a similar condition including this condition being imposed on the subsequent purchaser.

All rights reserved. Except for use in review, no part of this publication may be reproduced, stored in a retrieval system, or transmitted in any form or by any means, electronic, mechanical, photocopying, recording or otherwise, without the prior permission of the copyright owner.

Also by Judy Lawn

Novels
Progressions
Daisies Never Die
Watch Over Me

Short Story Collection
The Other Side of Solitude

Children's Picture Books
The Shrimp Who Wanted to be Pink
Sebastian's Tail
Jossie's New Home
Jamie's Monsters
I Want to Fly
One Haunted House

Young Adult
The Giant Greglusam
Timeboy Book One: Gondwana

Non-Fiction
Creative Writing
Take Heart & Write

Journal
Fashion Favorites

Contents

7	Introduction
9	**Chapter One:** Children's Picture Books
18	**Chapter Two:** Story Structure: Beginnings
28	**Chapter Three:** Story Structure: The middle
34	**Chapter Four:** Story Structure: The End
40	**Chapter Five:** Ideas
51	**Chapter Six:** Show Don't Tell
58	**Chapter Seven:** Dialogue
66	**Chapter Eight:** Pitfalls
77	**Chapter Nine:** A Complete Story
88	**Chapter Ten:** Publishing, Marketing and Selling
93	**Chapter Eleven:** Short Stories
100	**Chapter Twelve:** Putting Together *Nothing to Do*
109	**Chapter Thirteen:** Chapter Books
120	**Chapter Fourteen:** Internal Problem and Backstory
126	**Chapter Fifteen:** Transition Stage
133	**Chapter Sixteen:** Writing for Young Adults
143	**Chapter Seventeen:** Tone and Mood
154	**Top Points to Note When Choosing Characters**
155	**Conclusion**

156	Helpful Websites
157	About the Author
158	Bibliography

Introduction

Many elements make up a great children's book, some more important than others; all vital. These elements work together rather than as separate entities; one cannot exist without the other. I have begun with those I consider the most important; others may disagree with my choice.

All writing, in my opinion, begins with character; a strong protagonist readers can identify with and care about.

So, for the purposes of this book, I will begin with character.

Character, plot, setting, point-of-view, conflict, climax, pace, theme, tone, dialogue, voice, not to mention illustrations, editing, publishing and marketing; the list is long and can be confusing and oft-putting for beginners.

Some of you might think, "Surely you don't need all that for a children's book, especially a children's picture book? They must be easy to write being so short."

Oh, dear. There go several myths!

Children's picture books are difficult to write. (I'll explain in more detail in the following section; Children's Picture Books).

All fiction needs careful consideration of every one of the above elements, and more.

To bring all your elements together in a way that will appeal to both children and adults alike takes time, patience, thought, trial and error, and often endless re-writing. Occasionally, I've written a story quickly; when all the elements have come together the way I wanted them to. But more often than not I slog away day after day, week after week, before the story reaches anywhere near my expectations.

When my characters come to life and seem real to me–a joyous experience in a writer's life–when I can portray, in a few words, exactly what I want, when the story sings, that is a moment to savour; and everything a writer strives to achieve.

Another myth is that children will love every word you write. They won't. They'll squirm restlessly if the story doesn't hold their attention, or find a book they do like and ask you to read that one. Adults might offer false flattery and approval; children won't.

That said, don't be put off.

If you want to write a children's book, begin at once.

Begin with character.

CHAPTER ONE

Children's Picture Books

Character

As I mentioned in my introduction, children's picture books are difficult books to write.

Why? I hear you ask.

One of the reasons is because they are short; therefore, every word must count, must exist for the purpose of revealing character and plot, of moving the story forward. There is no room for a lengthy introduction, unnecessary description, too many characters, too much detail, repetition, and over-explanation.

The writer has less than a thousand words with which to tell the story. It must be engaging and entertaining, and appeal to both adults and children alike.

Adults buy children's picture books so they need to approve of the book they are purchasing; and the first thing they will look at is character:

1. Is this an interesting character?
2. What is the character's problem and do they solve it in a satisfying manner?
3. Are the illustrations appealing?
4. Is the story humorous and entertaining?
5. Is the moral of the story clear?
6. Will my child/grandchild enjoy this book?

Originality

It's not enough to have a great idea for a story about a child/bear/rooster/duck lost in the woods who happens upon a sleeping princess/engaging elf/pink elephant/yellow fluffy slippers. You are in danger of manufacturing a story out of snippets of stories you have either read before or heard about. You'll probably struggle to write the story and end up disappointed with your efforts.

You could also be accused of plagiarism.

Plots

There are only seven basic plots.

The Seven Basic Plots–Wikipedia

1. Overcoming the Monster
2. Rags to Riches
3. The Quest
4. Voyage and Return
5. Comedy
6. Tragedy
7. Rebirth

The way you present your **plots**, the multitudes of **plot-twists**, your **characters, settings, themes, tone, pace** and the **nuances** you bring to your stories will give your stories **originality**.

Choosing Original Characters

There are dozens and dozens of stories about fairies, witches, goblins, dwarfs, dragons and monsters, and just as many stories about ordinary everyday creatures like rabbits, dogs, cats, cows, pigs, sheep, bears, foxes, wolves, birds, guinea pigs, penguins and crickets.

So, how do you choose an **original** character?

You don't have to think of a creature/person/thing that has never been written about before, although if you *do* invent an exciting, original character never seen before, well done!

You can make an appealing, interesting, exciting character out of just about anything animate or inanimate, e.g. SpongeBob SquarePants.

Somehow, cockroaches don't make very appealing characters. Strangely, crocodiles and spiders do. There are also plenty of stories about snakes. It's all about **character**.

So, if you think you can make an appealing cockroach then go for it!

However, you *can* choose to write a story about an ordinary everyday creature/person/thing as long as you make your character original.

I've written children's picture books about a rat, a cow, a rabbit and a shrimp–all ordinary everyday creatures. What my characters do, how they react to the world around them, how they achieve their goals is what makes them **original**.

A Strong Protagonist

You need a **strong protagonist**, one the reader can immediately identify with and care about.

Think of your favourite children's picture book heroes/heroines: *The Three Billy Goats Gruff*, *The Three Little Pigs*, *Petunia*, *The Gingerbread Man*, *The Cat in the Hat*, *Where The Wild Things Are*, *Goodnight Moon*, *The Very Hungry Caterpillar*, *Thomas the Tank Engine*, *The Gruffalo*, *Hairy Maclary*, *Who Sank the Boat? The Littlest Reindeer*, and many, many more; unforgettable stories that are as popular today as when they were first published and all containing strong protagonists who will enthral children–and adults–for years to come.

These stories have stood the test of time because of their memorable protagonists.

I never forgot *Goodnight Moon*. My mother read me the story when I was a little girl; I later read it to my son and then my grandchildren. I also adored *The Littlest Reindeer*, *A Walk in the Forest* and *The Story of Ping*.

These fictional characters have delighted generations of readers and will continue to do so far into the future because they are **strong, original protagonists**.

Protagonist's Strengths and Flaws

Your protagonist needs to be a well-rounded, three-dimensional character with strengths and flaws. Make your characters real. No one is perfect. Readers don't like "Miss Goody Two Shoes." They'd like such characters to fall face-first into a mud puddle.

Children identify with a protagonist who gets into trouble, who makes mistakes, who says or does the wrong thing. As long as the protagonist redeems themselves at the end of the story in a satisfactory manner, children will be intrigued.

Anthropomorphism–the attribution of human characteristics or behaviour to animals or objects.

Anthropomorphism is as popular as ever in children's picture books. Children love animals with human characteristics; it allows them the chance to learn through the animals' adventures and challenges.

Examples: *The Three Little Pigs, Winnie-the-Pooh and his friends, Mickey Mouse, The Very Hungry Caterpillar, Fantastic Mr. Fox, Thomas the Tank Engine.*

You might like to Google the article entitled *The importance of anthropomorphism in children's picture books.* This discusses the origin of anthropomorphism with mention of *Aesop's Fables*, Beatrix Potter's *The Tale of Peter Rabbit*, and *Horton the Elephant* by Dr Seuss.

Exercise One

Make a list of your favourite children's picture book protagonists' memorable characteristics:

1. Their ability to solve problems.
2. To persevere where others have failed.
3. To lead so that others might follow.
4. To never give up no matter the improbability of the idea or the impossibility of the task.
5. To take on all adversity.

Extra Task: See if you can add to the above list.

The Protagonist's Problem

Without a problem for the protagonist to solve; a foe to defeat, an evil to thwart or an objective to strive for there is no story, nothing for the protagonist to learn/gain.

The protagonist uses his/her wits, skill, strength, courage and sometimes luck to achieve their objectives. Throughout the story, the protagonist usually encounters problems, danger, hardship and threats in many forms.

The protagonist needs to overcome each and every problem, threat, hardship and danger that arises before finally achieving their objective. In doing so, they learn valuable lessons about life, and themselves.

Theme

This is where the **theme**–or the idea of the story–comes from. The theme can usually be summed up in one word or a short phrase: trust, friendship, loyalty, courage or even a homily, "home is where the heart is." Stories might have more than one theme; and that is perfectly acceptable.

Our themes arise from our hobbies and interests, e.g. the environment, gardening, travel; and things that are important to us like trust, love, friendship and loyalty.

You can think about the theme before you write your story, or it may only become clear to you as you write, or when you examine your story afterwards.

Is your story about triumph over evil, or is it coming-of-age story where your protagonist learns something about themselves and the wider world.

The Three Billy Goats Gruff

If the three Billy goats did not have to outwit the troll to get to the field of fresh grass on the other side of the bridge, if there was no troll to try to stop them from achieving their goal then there would be no story, just three Billy goats strolling across a bridge on a sunny day to the field of grass on the other side.

Readers would feel let down by the story, disappointed there was nothing of significance to hold their attention.

The story needs a **problem** for the protagonists to solve; how do three Billy goats cross the river to where the juicy green grass is when a horrible troll controls the bridge; their only way of reaching the other side?

Readers need to wonder how the goats will succeed in attaining their objective and look forward to a good story that satisfies their curiosity. They will admire the two younger goats using their wits to outwit the troll and relish the troll meeting his watery end in his altercation with big Billy Goat.

What do you think the theme/s might be for *The Three Billy Goats Gruff*? When deciding on the theme/s you need to recall all the characters in the story not just the three Billy goats. What makes the troll act the way he does? What does this signify? Remember, the **theme** is the **idea** of the story, or what the story is about. Think of one word, or a short phrase, or a homily.

There can be more than one theme.

Extra Task: Read lots of children's picture books and try to figure out their appeal, what makes the story work.
Examine the **theme/s**.

Your Reader Needs to Care

Your reader needs to care about your protagonist from the outset, want them to win the battle, defeat the foe and achieve their objective. If the reader doesn't care, then your character is not strong enough to engage their attention. Or perhaps your protagonist's problem is not clearly defined?

Character Description

Description of your characters is not necessary in a children's picture book because there are illustrations of your protagonist/s and setting. But for the purposes of exercise two, describe your protagonist/s; it will help you to get to know your characters in more depth and what motivates them.

Exercise Two

1. Who is your protagonist?
2. Do you have an idea for a hero or heroine? Perhaps a name?
3. Jot down your ideas for your protagonist or make a list of characteristics.
4. Any thoughts on theme? It can be a rough outline at this stage.

Plot

Plot is what happens in the story–usually escalating conflict: something happens, then something else happens because of this and then something else happens after that, etc. This is your **plot**.

You can plot your story from the outset if you wish–many writers work this way–or work out your plot as you go along. Or perhaps you want to begin with a major scene and write from there. Use whatever method works for you. There is no right or wrong way to plot; only the way that works for you.

I tend to make up things as I go along, or begin with an idea/sentence/scene.

I will talk more about beginnings in a further chapter.

Exercise Three

1. Make a list of problems your protagonist might encounter.
2. Think of ways they might overcome their problems.
3. If one idea doesn't work out, don't be discouraged. Try another idea.
4. You will soon have your plot.

Chapter Two

Story Structure: Beginnings

Story structure largely consists of a **beginning** a **middle** and an **end**:

1. The **beginning** introduces the protagonist and outlines his/her problem.
2. The **middle** develops the story and shows the protagonist trying to solve their problem.
3. The **end** resolves the problem and brings all the elements of the story together in a satisfactory ending.

In fiction, you don't always need a happy ending but for a children's picture book it would be wise to present one.

This is not to say you can't write of gruesome events and characters. Many of the old fables and children's stories were filled with witches, goblins and giants, all bent on evil; think *Hansel and Gretel*. As long as events are resolved satisfactorily at the end of the story, children's stories can be about any subject. Hansel and Gretel outwitted the witch in the end.

Beginnings

Beginnings are often where writers struggle. It's no fun staring at a blank sheet of paper or a blank computer screen knowing you have a great idea, but not knowing how to begin your story.

There are many ways to begin. Following, are several examples from my children's picture books.

An engaging opening–one that takes the reader straight into the story.

Introduce your **protagonist** in the **first paragraph**, either with snappy dialogue or a short piece of description that quickly **sets the scene** and presents the **protagonist's problem**.

Below, is the opening of my first published children's picture book, *The Shrimp Who Wanted to be Pink* Reed Publishing (NZ) Ltd 2003

The little shrimp sat in the water beneath the mangrove trees with all the other shrimps and looked down at his semi-transparent body.

"This colour is no colour at all," he said. "I wonder what it would be like to be pink."

The other shrimps laughed.

"What a silly little shrimp," they said. "Semi-transparent is the best colour of all for a shrimp."

The **first paragraph** introduces the **protagonist** and identifies his **problem**. While the other shrimps laugh at the little shrimp, he is not deterred from setting out to discover what it would be like to be pink.

This makes the little shrimp a strong character; he is not afraid to follow his goal, to go out into the big wide world to seek his fortune, or, in this instance, to discover what it would be like to be pink. It might seem a foolish notion–and, indeed, it is–but through the little shrimp's adventures and discoveries, and the lessons he learns along the way, children learn that it's OK to try something new, that to venture into the unknown requires courage, but it can be done.

Children need to discover for themselves what happens when you "poke a finger in the flames." Ever tried to tell a child not to play with matches, or put their fingers in the fire/heater. Do they listen? Did we?

When the little shrimp wanders into danger–as indeed he must–he extracts himself by using his wits. So, children learn another lesson:

that if they do wander into danger, they have the ability to extract themselves by using their wits.

The story builds children's confidence: the little shrimp survived his journey/challenge/ordeal; they will, too.

Vocabulary and Big Words

Don't be afraid to use big words when writing for children. Children love big words. It's how they learn. Here, they learn a new word, semi-transparent, and also about camouflage. By discovering new words and their meanings children learn seamlessly.

That said, use realistic, age-appropriate language when writing for children. Use the words they use.

Make a Statement

I often try to make a **statement** with my **first sentence**. If you make a statement–a short one–this reduces the urge to waffle; to begin a long lengthy explanation of who your protagonist is, where they live, what they are doing and why, and how they came to be in this situation.

This is not necessary in a children's picture book, or, for that matter, any book IMO.

In the following examples of my children's picture books, study the opening sentences to see how the short, effective opening statement can be simply achieved.

Sebastian's Tail Penguin Group (NZ) 2008

Sebastian the rat was born without a tail. So he set out to find one.

Once again the **first paragraph** introduces the **protagonist** and identifies his **problem**.

Sebastian is a strong character. Born without a tail, Sebastian is up for the challenge of finding one. The reader knows nothing will deter Sebastian from his mission and look forward to joining him in his adventure.

Sebastian is ridiculed and ostracised by the other farmyard animals because he's different. Hurt, he retreats to lick his wounds. When he finds a friend, his enthusiasm for making a new tail returns. Together, with his new friend–always a contemporary and never an adult–Sebastian succeeds in making a tail that suits him.

Children learn from the story that even if they are different, there are those who will accept and like them for who they are without prejudice.

Jossie's New Home Jupiter Publishing NZ Ltd 2012/Judy Lawn 2016

Jossie the Jersey cow was tired of living in a paddock. So she went looking for a new home.

The **first paragraph** introduces the **protagonist** and identifies her **problem**.

Jossie's sudden dissatisfaction with her home and her search for a new one is universal; the other man's grass is always greener.

Jossie is a strong character. Her search for a new home leads her on a merry dance where every "home" she tries has something wrong with it. When she ends up back in her paddock–as most readers will have guessed she does–Jossie has come full circle; she has discovered for herself that the other man's grass is not greener after all. The theme "home is where the heart is" satisfies both children and adults alike.

Extra Details

The illustrations present a portrait of the protagonist, the setting and often other small **details** that add an extra dimension to the story.

In *Jossie's New Home*, the illustrations of the moon on every page, often peering in through a window or down from the night sky as he follows Jossie on her adventures acts as a catalyst for Jossie's emotions. There is no mention of the moon in the text; there doesn't need to be. This is where illustrations shine–a picture certainly does paint a thousand words.

Children soon spy these details and look for the moon on each page and laugh at the moon's absurd expressions.

In *Sebastian's Tail*, the first illustration shows Sebastian interacting happily with his parents in their comfortable family home, revealing to the reader that although Sebastian doesn't have a tail, his parents love him just as he is. It is his decision alone to go off in search of a tail.

Narrator's Voice and Tense

You need to decide whether to write in the present tense, "I" or the past tense, "he/she." The present tense is the character's voice; the past tense is known as the narrator's voice.

Sebastian's Tail

Present Tense/Character's Voice
"I haven't got a tail," said Sebastian. "I'm going to find one."

Past Tense/Narrator's Voice

Sebastian the rat was born without a tail. So he set out to find one.

The Shrimp Who Wanted to be Pink

You can use a mix of both character's and narrator's voices.

He went on down the river.

A sprat swam past. The sprat was a shimmering, shiny silver. Shimmering, shiny silver was a colourful colour, too. But the little shrimp still thought pink was better.

"What do you think of the colour pink?" he asked, startling the sprat who hadn't seen him.

"Pink would be the perfect colour for you," said the sprat. "Then I could see you and catch you and eat you!"

Try to keep the narrator's voice and, therefore, narrator intrusion to a minimum by staying in the character's thoughts. In the above excerpt even though it is the narrator's voice in the first two paragraphs, they are the little shrimp's observations/thoughts.

Rhyme and Rhythm

Many new writers try **rhyme** for their first attempts at a children's picture book, even though we often read that publishers don't want stories in rhyme. Why? I'm not sure of the exact reason, perhaps it's because they've read too many stories that don't rhyme exactly.

Rhyme is difficult to get right, but it must be right. To use a word, any word, just because it rhymes with the one you want is asking for trouble. It's worth taking the extra time to search for a word children will not only understand, but enjoy; and one that suits your protagonist and story.

Then there's the **rhythm** or the **music** of your story; making sure your sentences have a similar cadence and pattern so that when read aloud they flow and sound pleasing to the ear.

I've written stories that rhyme, usually ab, ab; first and third line rhyme, second and last line rhyme.

Jamie's Monsters Jupiter Publishing NZ Ltd 2015

Monsters lived at Jamie's place,
even in his tent.
They were always in his face,
everywhere he went.

The **first verse** introduces the **protagonist** and identifies his **problem**.

The phrase always in his face suggests that Jamie is not happy with the monsters.

The reader knows what the story will be about and wonders how Jamie will handle his "problem monsters." The illustration of Jamie rolling his eyes, holding his head in his hands and looking exasperated helps.

Through Jamie's adventures and interaction with the monsters, children learn that monsters need not always be scary and horrible.

The story helps children gain confidence of "dark and scary places." They learn that monsters can be befriended that they can be fun.

This story took me the longest to write. Finding suitable matching rhyming words that said what I wanted them to, and in the rhythm I wanted nearly drove me crazy! But with patience and persistence, loads of rewrites–and chocolate–I finally finished the book.

Below are two examples of my favourite verses:

Grisim on the stairs was mean,
he simply wouldn't budge.
Big and bad, grumpy and green,
he sat there like a lump of sludge.

Ringo on the roof was rude,
he made revolting burps!
He always sunbathed in the nude,
and drank his juice in slurps.

Children relish saying words like burps and slurps–onomatopoeia. They love rude, naughty characters; it gives them the freedom to giggle at the characters' behaviour, to be rude and naughty, too. (I guess I'm sticking my neck out with that statement; but I'm sure you know what I mean!)

Budge and sludge are great words for a story about monsters; remember what I said about finding the right words to suit your story and characters.

The multi-syllabic word revolting is also a good word for a story about monsters.

This is what is meant by painting a picture with words, and why it's vital to search for the right ones.

Examining the story now–isn't hindsight a wonderful thing–it might have sounded even better with he burped revolting burps and slurped his juice in slurps. Then again, that might be overdoing it! What do you thing?

Made is not a good word. The verbs drank, sunbathed and sat are stronger.

Alliteration

Alliteration is a wonderful device for children's picture books. I use it often.

Ringo on the roof was rude

The first, fourth and sixth words begin with the consonant *r* a wonderful letter to roll off the tongue, and, once again, great for a story about monsters.

Big and bad, grumpy and green

grumpy and green begin with the *g* consonant while big ends with the *g* consonant.
Big and bad is consonance–recurrence of sound–as is the beginning of grumpy and green–gru and gree.

There are lots of *m* sounds/consonants and consonance in the Grisim verse which help paint the picture of grumpy, lumpy Grisim who won't budge.
If a child has not heard the words budge or sludge before, he/she can work out the meaning from the context of the story and the illustrations of Grisim sitting in the middle of the stairs, like a lump of sludge, with Jamie glaring at him.

Vowel Sounds

The long vowel sounds, o, oo and u in Ringo, roof and rude are also wonderful to draw out and relish when reading the story out loud.

Exercise Four

1. Write a beginning sentence using the short statement method that introduces the protagonist and states his/her problem.
2. If you struggle with this method, write a longer sentence/paragraph introducing your protagonist and their problem then see if you can shorten it to one or two sentences.
3. Decide on voice and tense.
4. Try your hand at rhyme if you wish.
5. Remember to take your time and search for the right rhyming words.
6. Think about the rhythm, or music, of your story.

Chapter Three

Story Structure: The Middle

The **middle** develops the story and shows the protagonist trying different ways to solve his/her problem/s. Each attempt–which usually results in failure at this stage–deepens the story, and more often than not adds to the protagonist's problems.

Jossie's New Home

The barn looked interesting.
It was hot and stuffy and gave her hay fever.
The food was terrible–stale old straw!
Rats and mice ran about the barn all night long.
She didn't sleep a wink.

The orchard looked interesting.
It was cold and damp beneath the trees.
The food was terrible–too many green apples!
In the trees possums fought and chattered all night long.
She didn't sleep a wink.

The Protagonist's Main Mission/Problem–The Character Arc

The protagonist's main problem is what's known as the **character arc**, and will carry the story forward and not be resolved until near the end.

Jossie's main mission/problem is to find a new home, a place where she will be happy and comfortable for the rest of her life.

Peaks or Grey Spots

Each verse shows Jossie trying out a new home. None of them are quite right; posing the questions: will she ever sleep again? And, will she ever eat again?

While these two questions deepen the story–by adding to Jossie's problems–they don't detract from Jossie's main problem: will she ever find the right home? The main problem must stay to the forefront of the story and not be resolved until the end.

New problems are often referred to as **peaks** or **grey spots** in a story. They are usually resolved at that point and not revisited; as seen when Jossie tries the barn, the orchard and then the next place. Each place is deemed unsuitable in some way so Jossie must keep on searching for the right home.

Motivation

Jossie's search for a new home is the **motivation** that keeps the story moving forward; and readers turning the pages as they try to guess which place Jossie will try next, or whether she will end up back in her paddock.

The Wrong Choice

If Jossie chose the barn–the first place she tries–then the story would end there, almost before it had begun.

This decision is not strong enough to carry the story. Jossie has only tried one place and her decision to choose the barn lacks effort and endurance. It sounds like she is too lazy to try any other places. The barn will do even if it gives her hay fever and the food is terrible.

This makes Jossie a weak character, too tired and lazy to give her problem the attention it deserves.

Always allow your characters their story, their time to shine and solve their problems however long it takes and however difficult/nonsensical those problems are. Send them on a "perilous journey" enabling them to learn something about themselves, and life.

Repetition of Sentences and Phrases

Repetition of sentences and phrases in children's picture books and stories can be used to great effect; it's a literary device I often use.

In the above two verses of *Jossie's New Home*, Jossie is presented with a different home substitute in each new verse, while the end line, She didn't sleep a wink, is a statement children quickly learn to anticipate and repeat.

The repetition of the phrases: The food was terrible, and all night long work to anchor the story in the familiar. Children delight in repeating words and phrases. It teaches them to understand language. They love the anticipation/excitement of the next verse, knowing how it will end.

The last verse needs to be different, either a surprise or a play on words in the previous verses, but always a satisfying ending.

Transitioning From the Middle to the Next Stage

There is always a **transition stage** in every story, a moment when the adventure reaches a point when the central character must make a decision and answer the question: "what am I going to do about this situation/problem?"

It could be that your character needs to stand up to an opponent, fight for survival, or make a decision; usually one that will change his/her life forever.

This is known as the **transition stage** in the story, the lead up to the climax. Otherwise, the story would go on and on forever and be in danger of sinking under the weight of too much information.

For example, Jossie would keep trying out new homes, Sebastian would keep trying on yet another tail, the Little Shrimp would keep asking creatures what they thought of the colour pink.

Each story needs to reach the transition stage.

In *Jamie's Monsters*, Jamie decides he has had enough of the monsters and wants them to leave.

One day he shouted out loud, "Stop!
Stop the noise and all this fuss!
I've had enough of monsters, Stop!
You'll have to leave, get on the bus."

Now that Jamie has made his decision regarding the monsters, he must face the consequences of that decision.

At first he tells himself he's glad.

"I'm glad they've gone," Jamie said.
"I like the house this way.
I'm tired of every ugly head.
I hope the peace is here to stay."

However, as time goes by, Jamie misses the monsters and their noise, and decides he wants them back.

But then Jamie stopped to think,
what if he was far too late?
He looked for monsters green and pink,
as he hurried to the gate.

Asking Questions

Jamie wonders if by sending the monsters away he's left it too late to befriend them. Now he must work to get them back.

Often, your protagonist needs to reach the bottom/pit of despair before they can begin the climb back up to the top.

Always pose **questions** for your protagonists. Questions need answers. Questions and answers move the story forward.

If you get bogged down in the middle of your story and need to reach the transition stage, try asking questions or something of your protagonist that demands action.

The transition stage is easier to spot in *Jossie's New Home*.

The cow paddock looked interesting.

Jossie has come full circle in her search for a new home; back to the cow paddock. What will she do now? Jossie has to make a decision. The story has reached the **transition stage**.

In *Sebastian's Tail*, Sebastian comes to the end of trying out other creatures' tails when he spies a possum in the tree above him.

The possum had a long bushy brown tail.
Now there was a tail!
But Sebastian had already tried a long furry tail.
A possum's tail wasn't for him.
He sighed and tried to go to sleep.

Sebastian is impressed by the possum's tail but not enough to try it because he has already tried a long furry tail and it didn't work.

This is the point in the story when things change, the transition stage. What is Sebastian going to do now?

In *The Shrimp Who Wanted to be Pink*, the transition stage is when the little shrimp is caught by the children. He literally swims into danger. He wants to know what it's like to be pink and he's about to find out! What will he do now?

You will know when you have arrived at the transition stage if you can ask: what will my protagonist do now? It's decision time!

Exercise Five

1. Develop your story by writing several paragraphs deepening the story and showing how your protagonist might deal with his/her problem/s.
2. Take your time developing peaks and grey spots.
3. Use the literary devices; alliteration, onomatopoeia and repetition if you wish.
4. Have you reached the transition stage of your story?

Chapter Four

Story Structure: The End

The **end** of a story always resolves the protagonist's major problem.

As I mentioned in a previous paragraph, the ending must satisfy the reader. Everything that has gone before, all questions posed and problems presented in the story must be resolved here.

Climax and Resolution

The ending is always in two parts: the **climax** and the **resolution**.

The climax: often called the **black spot**.

The **climax** is where the protagonist faces his/her greatest challenge.

In fiction, the climax is often presented as a skirmish or a dramatic battle scene, but it can just as easily be a light bulb moment, or the final puzzle-piece clicking into place.

The climax must unfold quickly.

At this point in the story, the protagonist needs to win the battle, solve the problem, complete his journey and carry out his mission.

The resolution: the second part of the ending.

In this scene any lingering questions that have not been answered in the climax are answered here. You don't want your reader asking, "But what happened to that other character?"

There is usually no tension in the resolution; it is the "soft landing after the battle" and often presented as a victory celebration.

Jossie's New Home

The Climax

The cow paddock looked interesting.

Just as Jossie is running out of ideas for a new home, she spies the cow paddock–her old home; her final battleground. Will Jossie be happy returning to the cow paddock, a home she was once tired of or will she find the paddock wanting?

The Resolution Scene

The food was wonderful–sweet juicy grass!
Her bed on the ground was warm and cozy.
Other cows chewed their cud–a lovely lullaby.
Jossie slept soundly all night long.

Main Problem

Jossie's main problem, her search for a new home, is resolved.

Her other two problems, will she ever eat or sleep again, are also resolved.

There are no unanswered questions. The ending is satisfactory.

I often return at the end of the story to a phrase I've written in the beginning. It helps round out the story, to give it balance and strength.

In this instance, it's the play on the repeated phrases, The food was terrible, and She didn't sleep a wink. They become; The food was wonderful! And Jossie slept soundly all night long and add an amusing twist to the story.

The Shrimp Who Wanted to be Pink

The little shrimp has been captured by two children who have scooped him up in a yellow plastic bucket. He finds himself about to be barbecued by the children's father.

"We'll have a barbecue tonight," said the deep voice. "And we'll have shrimp for dinner. Roasted, toasted, pink shrimp!"
And then the little shrimp knew: only dead shrimps were pink!

This is the moment of clarity for the little shrimp. He wanted to be pink, and now he knows how foolish that idea was. He must save himself from certain death.

The Climax

The little shrimp knew that this was the end. He could hear the waves racing and dancing up the beach and he wanted, more than anything, to play with the waves.
So he took a huge, deep breath and gave the strongest, bravest flip of his semi-transparent tail and flipped right out of the brilliant-yellow plastic bucket. He landed with a "plop" on the wet, sandy beach and the cool waves gathered him back into the sea.

Motivation

The little shrimp's urge to once again "play with the waves" is what motivates him to escape. If he doesn't escape, he'll be barbecued. A strong motivation indeed!

But even though he has escaped a roasting, he is not safe yet. He still has to get past the sprat and the eel before he can reach the safety of home.

Resolution

The little shrimp was so happy to be back in the sea he danced and skipped for joy.
He heard the deep voice shouting, "Hey! The shrimp's gone!"
And then the little shrimp was swimming as fast as he could... past the sprat, who was asleep in the current... past the eel, who opened one beady eye... past the mud snail, who was snoring in his shell... to his home beneath the mangrove trees where all the other shrimps slept quietly beside the muddy river bank.
"Perhaps semi-transparent is the best colour for a shrimp after all," thought the little shrimp, and promptly fell asleep.

Once the little shrimp has successfully overcome his final two challenges–getting past the sprat and the eel–he is safe. There is no more tension. All his problems have been resolved in a satisfactory manner.

The resolution is often where you can keep the tension going, to a somewhat lesser degree, as long as the main problem has been resolved in the climax.

I have once again used the device of returning at the end of the story to something that happened in the beginning.

The theme might be belonging, or being happy in your own skin, or content with your life, or, simply, freedom; the freedom to play with waves, to sleep in your own bed, or to live with your fellow man. What do you think?

Sebastian's Tail

The Climax

They set to work, and soon Sebastian's new tail was finished.

The climax begins with the phrase: they set to work.
The questions posed are: will they be able to make a new tail? Will Sebastian be happy with his new tail?

The Resolution Scene

However, not all tension is resolved until Sebastian tries out his new tail and finds it to his liking.

He tried it on. It was the right length.
He swished it from side to side. It was the right weight.
He ran around the yard. His tail flowed behind him nicely.
He looked at his tail, and liked the colour.
"Thank you," he said to his new friend. "This is the right tail for me."
With his new friend watching, he danced round and round beneath the stars until he was dizzy with happiness.

Major Problem

Sebastian's major problem has been resolved; he has found/made a new tail and is happy with his tail; it is the right tail for him.
Along the way he has found a new friend; one who accepted him for himself from the beginning but who was happy to help him with his mission.

The Final Sentence

Although it might seem that the story has ended, there is still one final puzzle-piece to click into place.

And when he went out into the yard the next day, not one of the other animals had to ask him what he was.

Sebastian now "fits in." He looks like a rat because he has the right tail for a rat. None of the other animals question his identity. They accept him.
Sebastian's other problem has also been resolved.
There are no unanswered questions left. The ending is satisfactory.

Exercise Six

1. Write a satisfactory ending for your story, paying attention to the climax and the resolution scenes.
2. Make sure you have answered all questions and provided explanations of events.
3. Try to return at the end of the story to something you wrote in the beginning.
4. Add an amusing twist in the final paragraph/sentence if you can.

Chapter Five

Ideas

People often ask me, "Where do you get your ideas from?"
    The truth is, ideas are everywhere:

1. In the world around us.
2. Our homes and workplaces.
3. Memories of childhood.
4. Places we visit.
5. People we met.
6. Books we read.
7. Movies, magazines, television, social media; the list is endless.

Setting

Never be restricted by **setting**. Settings can be anywhere as long as your protagonist "fits the scene" as it were.

The setting itself becomes as much a character as the protagonist, and should play a major role in the story.

Think of the forest setting in *Hansel and Gretel*, or the grassy paddocks in *The Three Billy Goats Gruff*. Would those stories have worked as well in a different setting? The answer is no; the setting played a vital role in the story.

Try imagining the three Billy goats in the city. Or Hansel and Gretel at the seaside, or Little Red Riding Hood in an apartment. The settings are not quite right, are they?

But you might get an idea for a different story.

Ideas for Children's Picture Books

Ideas for children's picture books spark places like: farms, zoos, parks, the countryside and the beach; a place where I get many of my ideas. Equally, the city and city life, high-rise buildings, ports, harbours, train/bus stations, historic buildings, and your local neighbourhood all provide settings for children's picture books.

Spend a day at one of these places and observe what happens. Take a notebook or your phone and make/record notes. I'm sure you'll come up with plenty of ideas.

Make a List

The Shrimp Who Wanted to be Pink evolved from my love of the sea, and a childhood spent exploring rock pools and beaches, and my many fishing excursions.

1. I made a list of characters and places I might use in the story: beach, rock pool, shells, seaweed, crabs, seahorses, starfish, shrimp, eel, mud snail, sprat, river, old post, children, bucket, driftwood, fire, waves, etc.
2. Then I thought about the colours of the characters; the semi-transparent shrimp, the shimmering shiny silver sprat and the muddy brown eel and snail.
3. Next, I thought about the colours of the sea, the river and the beach.
4. It doesn't matter if you don't use everything on your list; it's a collection of your ideas, a place to start.

The idea for *Jossie's New Home* evolved from my days of helping out on my aunt's farm with the milking and getting to know her wonderful gentle Jersey cows.

I began compiling my list: barn, orchard, dog kennel, hen house, garage, paddock, cow shed, grass, apples, pigs, possums, rats, mice, straw, hay, trees, pigsty, etc.

Send Your Protagonist on a Journey

1. Imagine your protagonist setting out on a journey to conquer their foes, face their fears, solve their problem/s, which bring them satisfaction and perhaps acclaim. "Once Upon a Time" should be avoided at all cost IMO.
2. For *Jossie's New Home* I pictured the layout of my aunt's farm and the different places a cow might think of as a suitable home.
3. Then I imagined Jossie setting off on her journey, trying these "homes," and finding each one unsatisfactory.
4. I had to think of a reason why each place would be unsatisfactory.
5. That was how I got my story, my plot.

Sebastian's Tail begins with Sebastian's journey; he sets out to find a new tail. Again, I had to picture the other animals/characters Sebastian might meet along the way, and began my list: Mrs Williams, feather duster, blackbird, sheep, lamb, rooster, puppies, skink, pig, possum, rat, trees, grass, moon, rope, plastic, barn, yard, etc.

Jamie's Monsters is a home setting; Jamie's home. I had to picture each monster, and present each monster as a "problem monster" for Jamie. The monsters needed to be somewhere in the house; and so my list began: Jamie, monsters, bedroom, stairs, roof, rubbish bin, wardrobe, laundry tub, bus, gate, party, cakes, dancing, sunlight, balloons, etc.

But the general idea of an adventure for the protagonist was still my main impetus for the story.

A One to Ten Numbers Book

1. For my one to ten numbers book, *One Haunted House*, Judy Lawn 2017 I decided on a haunted house theme, but with cute critters.
2. I began my list: haunted house, doors, windows, roof, chimney, cats, rats, bats, pumpkins, spiders, ghosts, skeletons, balloons, stars, etc.
3. Next, I had to work out the order for my creatures to appear.
4. A numbers book needs to be more than a numbered list of things/places/people; there needs to be something happening (plot) and, as always, a why (theme).
5. The setting is the haunted house on Hurricane Hill, with several scenes set in the interior of the house, others outside.
6. The main protagonist is the haunted house.
7. I decided that the haunted house imagines he is all alone on Hurricane Hill, unaware at first of his surprising guests; the critters who live in and around the house. At the end of the story he makes friends with them and is no longer alone or lonely.
8. And so I had my storyline, my plot.
9. I liaised with my illustrator via the internet as she lived in Italy; and she came up with wonderful illustrations.
10. I decided to use alliteration in each verse.

Three Verses from *One Haunted House*

One haunted house high on Hurricane Hill.

Three hairy spiders hang out and hide.

Nine gleeful ghosts gaze in through the gates.

The final scene in the book shows the haunted house and his guests enjoying a "spooky party" on Hurricane Hill–a literal and figurative coming together of all the characters.

Write a Short Back Cover Blurb for Your Story

Try writing a short back cover blurb for your story revealing your protagonist's problems and how they are might approach solving them. There's no need to reveal everything; always leave an intrigue for the reader.

Back Cover Blurb for *One Haunted House*:

Haunted House is all alone on Hurricane Hill.
Or is He?
Who else lives nearby?
Are they friend or foe?
When nine gleeful ghosts gaze in through the gates, what should Haunted House do? They look friendly, but can he trust them?
Will Haunted House ever make friends with his surprising guests?

I have mentioned asking questions previously: ask a question and you will always get an answer. Be patient.

Back cover blurb for *Sebastian's Tail*:

Sebastian is a rat with a problem; he has no tail. Try as he might he just can't find the right tail for him. They're either too long or too curly, or even too fluffy.

Just when he has given up, help arrives.

Back cover blurb for *Jamie's Monsters*:

Monsters are everywhere at Jamie's Place. They get in his way, they wreck things, they make a mess and they keep him awake at night. The monsters are so loud and bad they make Jamie's poor head thump! So Jamie sends the monsters away.

"You'll have to leave. Get on the bus!" he tells them.

But has Jamie made the right decision? When he discovers how lonely he is on his own, he decides to change his mind.

Will Jamie be too late, or will the monsters come back when Jamie calls them?

Back cover blurb for *Jossie's New Home*:

Jossie the Jersey cow is tired of living in a paddock–so she goes off in search of a new home. She tries the orchard, the dog kennel, the hen house, and even the garage, only to discover she can't sleep a wink.

Just when Jossie is wondering what else to try, and if she will ever sleep again, she spies the perfect place!

Keep a Notebook/Record on Your Phone

If you are stuck for ideas, start keeping notes of things you find interesting or think of when you are out and about, on your phone or in a notebook. Ask yourself questions; if you ask a question, you will always find an answer.

Take photographs of animals, plants, insects or local events happening in your neighbourhood.

Become a people watcher. This is fun and you can often find ideas from things people do and say.

Listen to conversations. Did I say that? Yes! I always tell people, "Be careful what you tell me. I might write about it."

Obviously, keep within respectful, legal restrictions.

Write What You Know

You might have heard the phrase "**write what you know**." There's a lot of truth in it. For starters, you will be confident writing about things you are interested in or have a sound knowledge of, and settings you are familiar with.

Knowledge of your subject adds authenticity to your stories.

My lifetime study of the sea and the creatures that inhabit rock pools, my days of catching shrimps, of putting my arms in the water and watching them drift over to investigate and touch my skin with their tiny legs and sharp little horns, aided in my writing a story about a shrimp. I know what they look like, how they feel, how they smell, how they act.

We can research our subject/s, but nothing replaces raw experience of people, places and things.

That said, don't be put off tackling a subject you are not familiar with. You might be surprised by what you learn and discover information for several books.

Don't guess what a thing might be like, or rely on what people tell you or "the common belief." Research your subject.

How to and Problems to Solve

Think of problems your protagonist/s might face; everyday problems that occur in daily life:

1. How do the children get to school when the car breaks down?
2. How do the children cope when Mum gets sick and Dad's at work?
3. What do the children do when the family pet dies?
4. How do children cope when a grandparent dies?
5. What do children do when they come face to face with a dangerous animal?
6. Why should children go to bed when they want to stay up and watch TV?
7. Which is best, public school or home school?
8. When should children get their first job?

Extra Task: see if you can add to the above list.

The Problems Facing Humankind:

1. What will we do with all the rubbish collecting in the oceans?
2. How should we save our endangered species?
3. What to do in a hurricane?
4. Where to go when there's an earthquake?
5. How to stay calm in a storm?
6. What to do in a fire?
7. What should we do about climate change?

Extra Task: see if you can add to the above list.

Questions Children Ask

Children all seem to go through a stage of asking endless questions. One day my three-year-old son, after asking questions all day long which I struggled to answer, finally finishing up with, "Mum, how many fish live in the sea?" To say I was floored is an understatement!

But it did get me thinking. I later wrote a story attempting to answer the question, but wasn't happy with the finished piece. I may go back to it one day.

By listening to questions children ask you might get an idea for a story.

Fun Questions Children Might Ask:

1. Why do children believe in monsters?
2. Why is the sky blue?
3. How do fish sleep?
4. Why is the moon yellow?
5. What is the moon made of?
6. Will people ever live on the moon?
7. How do planes fly?
8. What are clouds made of?
9. Where do butterflies go in winter?
10. Why are the stars so bright?
11. How many planets are there?
12. Do people live on the other planets?
13. Are giants real?
14. Can I be a fairy/elf/wizard?

Extra task: see if you can add to the above list.

Idioms of Improbability

You might find an idea for a children's picture book from well-known idioms of improbability like:

1. Once in a blue moon
2. The cow jumped over the moon
3. When pigs fly
4. Hit the ceiling
5. It costs an arm and a leg
6. As scarce as hen's teeth

Number of Words

With so few words to play with in a children's picture book there is no room for a lengthy introduction; you need to plunge immediately into the story.

As to the word count, keep it well under 1000 words. 600 words is a better target, or even less.

It's no good saying, "Oh, but my story is much longer. I couldn't possibly cut any words." You can and you must:

1. Cut out all the boring bits.
2. Shorten long, repetitious sentences.
3. Remove dialogue that repeats what you've said in the text.
4. Remove those extra characters that don't have any real place in the story.
5. Reduce your scenes.
6. Delete everything that is not necessary to move the story forward.

Make Every Word Count

If a word is not doing its job to reveal another aspect of your character, move the story forward, entertain, then it has no place in your story. Remove it!

Read Your Story Out Loud

Read your story **out loud**, several times. You'll soon hear the repetition; the phrases and words you've repeated without being aware of doing so.

Reading your story out loud lets you hear how it might be read by children and adults. You will get a sense of how the story flows, and hear any awkward words that might "trip up the tongue" and, therefore, need changing or deleting.

Exercise 7

1. There's no need to be stuck for ideas; start building your "ideas list" now.
2. Name three places you visited recently, and any ideas for a children's picture book that come to mind.
3. Picture yourself in the setting and recall things that caught your attention and events that happened while you were there.
4. Try placing your protagonist in the setting and think of a problem they need to solve.
5. Read your story out loud.
6. First editing session. See if you can reduce the number of words in your manuscript without detracting from the story of taking anything away from your character's journey.

Chapter Six

Show Don't Tell

Show your protagonist/s in action, thereby revealing their character. **Don't tell** your audience that the little shrimp had an inquisitive nature, and it was this aspect of his nature that often led him into trouble.

Apart from that being a ghastly sentence, you don't want to say anything like that in a children's picture book, or, for that matter, any book!

You are telling your readers what to think of your protagonist, instead of allowing them to work out your protagonist's nature for themselves.

The Shrimp Who Wanted to be Pink

The little shrimp swam over to an eel, who was lying in a long muddy brown line in the muddy brown mud.

"Wouldn't you like to be pink?" asked the little shrimp.

"Mmm, let me see," said the eel, watching the little shrimp through his beady, black eyes.

He came closer.

Too close!

The little shrimp darted away.

Show the little shrimp being inquisitive. **Show** the little shrimp noticing the eel watching him from beady, black eyes. **Show** the little shrimp escaping from the eel with liveliness and courage.

If the little shrimp didn't notice how the eel was behaving–and, therefore, escape–the eel would gobble him up and that would be the end of the story.

Whilst this underlies the "stranger danger" theme, it also teaches children to be aware of how others act, and to learn to read the signs of danger and take note of what is happening in the world around them; to be alert. Once again, they learn through the shrimp's actions that by using their wits they, too, can escape danger.

In the next scene the little shrimp asks the same question of a sprat.

He went on down the river.

A sprat swam past. The sprat was a shimmering, shiny silver. Shimmering, shiny silver was a colourful colour too. But the little shrimp still thought pink was better.

"What do you think of the colour pink?" he asked, startling the sprat who hadn't seen him.

"Pink would be the perfect colour for you," said the sprat. "Then I could see you and catch you and eat you!"

The little shrimp sprang away and hid behind an old brown post in the brownish, green water. And because he was semi-transparent, he looked like part of the old post. The sprat couldn't see him and swam away in disgust.

In this segment, the little shrimp once again reveals his adroitness in escaping from danger. But his escape is largely due to the fact that he is semi-transparent and the sprat can't see him hiding behind the post.

The little shrimp may not be aware of his advantage of being semi-transparent–he still wants to be pink–but readers will. This underlines the theme: be proud of who you are, learn to be happy in your own skin or work with what you've got.

Repetition and Alliteration

I use **repetition** and **alliteration** in my stories; they are my favourite literary device.

By repetition I mean the deliberate repetition of words and phrases for effect, not the overuse of words or sentences. Alliteration is also deliberate.

Shimmering shiny silver is repeated in the above excerpt for effect. The little shrimp wants to be pink, so he notices the colour of other sea creatures: the mud snail, the eel and the sprat.

Sebastian's Tail

Sebastian the rat was born without a tail. So he set out to find one.
The first thing he saw when he emerged from his hole was Mrs Williams dusting.
Sebastian stared at the bright pink feathery duster.
Now that would be a tail!
The moment Mrs Williams put down the duster, Sebastian scampered into the room.
It took him quite a while to extract some feathers from the duster and make a tail.
But what a tail!
He strutted around feeling very pleased with himself.
"What are you?" asked the blackbird.
"I'm a rat," said Sebastian.
"With that tail?" The blackbird flew away screeching with laughter.
Just then Sebastian heard another screech. Mrs Williams had spotted Sebastian with his pink feathery tail. She came after him with a big broom!
Sebastian pulled off his tail and ran for his life!

Don't tell your readers that Sebastian was an adventurous and courageous little fellow with a cheerful disposition, and not afraid of thinking for himself.

1. **Show** Sebastian being adventurous.
2. **Show** Sebastian looking at the pink feathery duster and wondering if the feathers might make a great tail.
3. **Show** Sebastian waiting for Mrs Williams to put down the duster and exit the room. Only when all danger has passed does he emerge from the safety of his home to scamper over to the duster and extract feathers for his tail. What does this reveal of his character?
4. **Show** Sebastian being proud of his effort.
5. **Show** Sebastian being hurt by the blackbird's laughter.
6. **Show** Sebastian escaping from Mrs Williams and her broom.

The theme is about "fitting in." Sebastian wants to be like all the other animals with tails that suit them. His search will lead him on many adventures until he finds the right tail for him.

Themes are there for readers to discover or think about. Allow your readers to make up their own minds about your characters and the reasons for their actions.

Passive versus Active

By telling your readers how your protagonist feels you are writing in the **passive**.

By **showing** your characters in action you are writing in the **active**.

Saving the Day

Your **protagonist** must always be the one to **escape danger**, think his way out of a difficult situation or **save the day**.

In children's picture books it can never be the adult in the story–if there is one. It must always be your protagonist, or a contemporary.

This reinforces children's perception that, with a bit of effort/willpower or using their wits they, too, can escape danger, think their way out of a difficult situation or save the day.

It's what makes a story powerful and empowering.

Examine the protagonist's journeys in the children's picture books and stories you know. You'll discover that the protagonist always outwits the evil giant/escapes from the dungeon/saves the day.

The Three Billy Goats Gruff

In *The Three Billy Goats Gruff* the goats outwit the troll by using their wits to make the troll look foolish.

They appeal to the Troll's greed–his weakest point–and use the Troll's greed of wanting a bigger and better meal to outwit him. In doing so, the three Billy goats achieve their goal, which is to escape the troll and cross the river to where the tastier grass grows.

The troll is left languishing in the river contemplating his foolishness and belatedly realising that the little Billy goat would have made a small but tasty dinner, and so would have the middle-sized Billy goat. But because he wanted "the biggest dinner of all" he now has no dinner.

The troll's eyes were too big for his stomach; a feeling those of us who have ever over-indulged at the dinner table may recognise.

Never Talk Down to Children

Children will soon let you know if they think the story you're reading them isn't up to scratch. They'll wriggle away, or tell you, "That's a boring story" or "I don't like that story."

Children can detect a false story and false tone at a hundred paces.

While they might be amused at dialect or character's voices, unless the character is likeable and well-rounded and honestly attempting to solve a problem children can identify with they will lose interest in the story no matter how entertaining you try to be.

Keep your prose straightforward and honest as if you were talking to a child and retelling an interesting/amusing/entertaining/serious incident or explaining a character's struggles in finally achieving their goal.

Everyone loves a winner, especially children. They will fall in love with a character who strives to attain a higher knowledge of life–no matter how serious/ridiculous the situation or struggle–as long as the character is portrayed as one who does his/her best and keeps on trying until they achieve a satisfactory outcome.

Endings

Your story doesn't need a spectacular ending with stars exploding and your protagonist exalting on a solid gold throne.

Simple adventures and stories about everyday life offer equal opportunity for genuine and honest endings.

But your protagonist does need to climb the highest mountain, sail the seven seas, fight their way through the thickest jungle, journey to a distant planet, solve the problem/puzzle and find the treasure; they cannot give up half-way through their adventure because it's too hard. Heroes don't give up; they keep going no matter the hardship.

Exercise 8

1. Write a story showing your protagonist/s in action.
2. Don't tell your reader about your protagonist by describing their characteristics; allow your reader to make up their own minds about your protagonist/s.
3. Write in the active, not the passive.

Chapter Seven

Dialogue

Use **dialogue** whenever you can to reveal the protagonist's intentions and emotions.

A mix of both narrative and dialogue, usually one third narrative, one third dialogue and one third introspection (protagonist's inner thoughts) will help with the pace of your story. Dialogue is easier to read than pages of narrative which slow down your story.

Use dialogue that children use. Dialogue that belongs to a bygone era has no place in a modern children's picture book–unless you are writing a historical story, and then the dialogue would have to be correct for the era you choose.

If your story warrants the use of colloquial language or swear words, then use that language as long as it's something your protagonist would say.

The Shrimp Who Wanted to be Pink

>The little shrimp found a mud snail that was the colour of mud.
>"Don't you think pink would be a good colour to be?" the shrimp asked.
>The mud snail just smiled. "The colour of mud is the right colour for me," he said, and crawled away.

Sebastian's Tail

>The rat looked at Sebastian. "What sort of a tail do you want?"
>Sebastian thought about all the tails he had seen so far.
>"Not too big, but not too small either," he said. "Curvy, but not curly, sleek but not shiny, and definitely not furry or feathery or brightly coloured."

Both segments have a balanced mix of narrative and dialogue.

Dialogue is not always an absolute necessity in a children's picture book–and I can hardly believe I've stated that as I always advocate using dialogue where possible over exposition.

Jossie's New Home is devoid of dialogue. Granted, the short verses are introspection; Jossie's inner thoughts. The reader sees everything and experiences everything through Jossie's eyes. The first line in each segment; The barn/orchard/pigsty looked interesting, is Jossie's thoughts. The reader, along with Jossie, examines the barn/orchard/pigsty etc. and wonders if it will make a suitable home.

Verbs and Colour Words

Use plenty of **verbs**; action words, or what I call **colour words** in your stories; words that paint pictures, reveal character and move the story forward.

Beware of too many adjectives which can slow down your story and make it ordinary.

The lovely cake is a boring, everyday description.

The cake needs to scrumptious, scrummy, or delish; words children understand and relish repeating.

Jamie's Monsters

Wallace in the wardrobe squeezed
into Jamie's brand new jeans.
But then he coughed and sniffed and sneezed,
and POP! He burst the seams!

Children love words and phrases like, POP, and He burst the seams!

If you are struggling with how to introduce dialogue into your story, try having your protagonist ask a question. Study the examples above in *The Shrimp Who Wanted to be Pink* and *Sebastian's Tail*.

Instead of passive description; the water was warm, give your character a voice, and write in the active; "Where's your red-and-white polka-dot bikini, Lilly?"

Converting Your Narrative into Dialogue

Convert your narrative into dialogue by having your characters describe their actions and intentions.

Make sure your dialogue moves the story forward and says something pertaining to theme, or references the protagonist's problem. Dialogue shouldn't exist if it's not necessary to the story.

Sebastian's Tail

Narrative

Sebastian and his new friend set to work making a new tail for Sebastian out of some rope, string and grey plastic they found in the barn.

Sebastian began to feel enthusiastic again.

Dialogue

"We could make one from this rope here and the grey plastic I saw in the barn," said the rat.

"And tie it together with this string!" Sebastian said, beginning to feel enthusiastic again.

Jamie's Monsters

Narrative

Jamie wanted the monsters to come back and wished he hadn't sent them away. He'd made a mistake, but what could he do?

Dialogue

"Please come back!" he yelled out loud.
"Please come home, I miss you all.
I'd like to see one happy crowd,
of Monsters big and Monsters small!"

The Five Senses: Taste, Touch, Sight, Sound, Smell

Too often in stories there is little or no mention of either taste or smell. By mentioning both, either directly or indirectly, you add depth and grit to your stories.

Jossie's New Home

It was hot and stuffy and gave her hay fever.
The food was terrible–stale old straw!

Can you smell the stuffy barn and taste the stale old straw? Does your mouth feel dry and gritty? Do you want to sneeze or cough?

The verse is a mix of both direct and indirect mention of smell and taste. You don't always have to say; the barn smelt stuffy, or the food tasted terrible.

Jamie's Monsters

Gilby in the rubbish bin,
ate every slimy scrap!
From rotten fish to chicken skin,
they slithered to his lap!

This rhyming verse certainly speaks for itself, aided and abetted by the illustration of the monster happily scoffing a fish bone, and dribbling.

This is indirect mention of smell and taste.

The alliteration slimy scrap and the verb slithered aid in painting a portrait of a monster who might live in a rubbish bin.

The Shrimp Who Wanted to be Pink

The children gathered driftwood and soon, through the yellow bucket, the little shrimp could see fire!

This is another example of indirect mention of smell and taste; and in this instance, sight and sound, too. Can you smell the driftwood smoke? Taste it? Can you hear the sound of the fire crackling and feel the heat of the flames?

Taste, smell, sight, sound and touch can all be revealed in simple ways without saying, the driftwood smoke smelt tangy, or the fire made an angry crackling sound.

Always reveal the **five senses** through the eyes of your protagonist. Don't forget the sixth sense.

Exercise Nine

1. Examine your dialogue.
2. Is it fresh and crisp?
3. Does it move the story forward?
4. If your story is bogged down in too much narrative, try converting parts of the narrative into dialogue.
5. Use the five senses in your story, sight, sound, taste, touch, smell.
6. Don't forget the sixth sense.

External and Internal Problems

Most stories will contain both an **external problem**–the hero's physical journey or search, and an **internal problem**–the hero's spiritual journey/journey of self-discovery.

One cannot exist without the other.

In *Jossie's New Home*, Jossie's **external problem** is finding a new home.

Her **internal problem** is her desire to find a home where she will be happy and content, somewhere that will satisfy her soul.

When Jossie finally finds her perfect home, she discovers the place where she is most happy and content is her old home, the cow paddock.

Both Jossie's **external** and **internal** problems are resolved.

Jossie has learnt that the grass is not greener on the other side after all–the stories message or theme.

The Shrimp Who Wanted to be Pink

In *The Shrimp Who Wanted to be Pink*, the external problem and the internal problem are closely linked. The little shrimp's search to discover what it would be like to be pink–his **external problem**–leads him further and further from the comfort and familiarity of his home, and into danger. His **internal problem** is to accept himself, to learn to live in his own skin.

The first creature he confronts is a mud snail, an unthreatening, benign creature. The eel, however is an entirely different creature and threatens the little shrimp's life; as does the sprat. But when the little shrimp is caught by the children playing at the beach, he is in grave danger. He has reached the pinnacle of his search–to discover what it would be like to be pink–and now must face the consequences of his actions; an ultimate test of his endurance as he fights for his life.

When he finally escapes and returns to his home in the river, he has learnt a hard but truthful lesson; be happy in your own skin, and, home is the best place of all.

Both his **external** and **internal** problems have been resolved.

Jamie's Monsters

Again, both the external and internal problems are closely related. Jamie's **external problem** is what to do about the monsters. His **internal problem** is to overcome his annoyance of the monsters and accept them as friends, thereby accepting himself.

Or perhaps the monsters exist only in Jamie's imagination? Most children imagine a monster hiding under the bed or in the wardrobe at some stage of their young lives. Therefore, Jamie's **internal problem** is overcoming the fear of "dark and scary places."

Exercise Ten

1. Have you included both the internal and external problem/s for your protagonist?
2. If your protagonist's external problem is clear but the internal problem seems elusive or even non-existent, examine the story again and try to tie in an internal problem relevant to your protagonist's external problem.
3. Think of the internal problem as your protagonist's inner search for the truth or a spiritual journey.

Chapter Eight

Pitfalls

Pitfalls to be Aware of in Beginnings

I might have begun Sebastian's Tail thus:

> When Sebastian the rat was born, he noticed that he had no tail.
> "Oh, woe is me!" cried Sebastian. "I haven't got a tail!"
> Sebastian wondered why he didn't have a tail when all his brothers and sisters had one. What had he done? Tears filled his eyes as he crept away to hide.
> "It's because I've been a bad rat." He sniffed, feeling more miserable than ever. "That's why I don't have a tail."
> "Go and play with your brothers and sisters, Sebastian," said his mother.
> "Yes, come and play, Sebastian," smirked his youngest sister.
> "I don't want to play," sobbed Sebastian. "I haven't got a tail. I'm very unhappy."
> "Don't be silly, Sebastian," said his mother. "I'm sure we can make you a tail."

You might think the beginning sounds fine. You might even feel sorry for Sebastian.

However, the beginning is far too long and full of unnecessary repetition–the fact that Sebastian doesn't have a tail is mentioned five times. Sebastian is fast becoming an annoying, unsympathetic, self-absorbed character. That might seem a harsh assessment, but it's the truth. No one likes a "moaning mini."

He is not a strong protagonist as he makes no attempt to think of a solution to his problem which is what a strong protagonist would do. Readers expect to find a hero, someone they can look up to and admire for their courage and ingenuity in the pages of a children's picture book.

Feeling more miserable than ever followed by He sniffed, is a repetition of his action, and unnecessary. The writer is telling the reader how Sebastian feels, not showing them. I'm very unhappy, is more unnecessary repetition. Ditto, sobbed Sebastian followed by, I'm very unhappy. The reader knows Sebastian is unhappy. They don't need to be told again and again. They are likely to throw this book across the room in disgust.

More Mistakes

When Sebastian the rat was born, he noticed that he had no tail.
"Oh, woe is me!" cried Sebastian. "I haven't got a tail!"

The second sentence is an unnecessary repetition of the first–using dialogue to repeat what was explained in the narrative.

Delete that it's not needed. Sometimes "that" is necessary but usually it can be deleted.

Sebastian wondered why he didn't have a tail when all his brothers and sisters had one. What had he done? Tears filled his eyes as he crept away to hide.

The above sentence is passive. The sentence needs to be active. To achieve this, write Sebastian's thoughts:

"Why haven't I got a tail like my brothers and sisters," Sebastian wondered? "What have I done?" Tears filled his eyes and he crept away to hide.

A Redundancy

More miserable than ever is a redundancy. Miserable is sufficient.

While the protagonist's problem is revealed–six times–a solution is not presented.

The reader is not interested in Sebastian's smirking youngest sister who doesn't even have a name.

The story sounds righteous. There is a lot of "writer intrusion" with the writer telling the reader how Sebastian feels.

No modern child would understand the phrase Oh, woe is me.

Sebastian's mother seems the strongest character as she is going to solve Sebastian's problem for him–an absolute no, no in a children's picture book.

The protagonist must solve the problem, not the adult.

Condense all that nonsense into one or two sentences that reveal Sebastian's problem and present his search for a solution.

Sebastian the rat was born without a tail.
So he set out to find one.

The Shrimp Who Wanted to be Pink

I might have begun the story thus:

The little shrimp sat in the water beneath the mangrove trees with all the other shrimps. He was feeling a bit miserable today. And it was all because of his colour–or lack of colour, because semi-transparent was no colour at all.

"This colour is no colour at all," he moped, looking down at his semi-transparent body. "I wish I was some other colour. Maybe pink? Or, blue, or yellow or purple or brindle." The little shrimp had heard of the colour brindle. He didn't know what colour brindle was, but it sounded like it might be a good colour. Although, perhaps not. It wasn't much good choosing to be a colour that he didn't really know.

The other shrimps were laughing at him. He poked out his tongue. What did they know? They thought it was OK to be semi-transparent, but the little shrimp didn't want to be semi-transparent. He wanted to be pink. Or maybe blue or yellow? He couldn't decide which colour to choose.

Again, the beginning is too drawn out–most of it redundant. There is too much repetition. (I've overdone things to show you what to avoid).

The writer is telling the reader how Sebastian feels and why.

"He was feeling a bit miserable today. And it was all because of his colour–or lack of colour, because semi-transparent was no colour at all."

The problem of Sebastian's colour is now dragged out until it becomes unbearably boring. Who cares about brindle or blue or yellow? The word colour is mentioned eleven times. Gag!

The protagonist should never mope, be rude or indecisive. He is not a strong protagonist. He's a sulky pain in the butt! What is his problem again? Who cares? This is a boring story.

Condense that repetitive rubbish to one or two sentences, or a short paragraph introducing the protagonist and stating his problem with a hint of what he might do to solve the problem.

The little shrimp sat in the water beneath the mangrove trees with all the other shrimps and looked down at his semi-transparent body.

"This colour is no colour at all," he said. "I wonder what it would be like to be pink."

The other shrimps laughed.

"What a silly little shrimp," they said. "Semi-transparent is the best colour of all for a shrimp."

There is no need for a question mark after pink as it is a rhetorical question.

Jossie's New Home

I might have begun the story thus:

Jossie the Jersey cow frowned at the cow paddock and all the other cows chewing their cud. What a boring place the cow paddock was, she thought. Nothing ever happened. It was boring. She didn't want to live here anymore.

"I don't like living here," she said to her neighbour, a rather fat and lazy cow that Jossie didn't even really like much. "I'm going to leave the cow paddock and find somewhere else to live. This place is so boring."

"Really?" Her neighbour chewed her cud contentedly. "Where will you go?"

"I haven't thought yet." Jossie sighed heavily. "But there must be some place better than a boring old cow paddock."

Once again, far too much repetition in the opening paragraphs. Jossie says/thinks the paddock is boring at least five times. The dialogue is mostly a repetition of Jossie's thoughts.

The main protagonist should never act/sound petulant or disgruntled, or be bitchy. Jossie is not a strong protagonist. Readers are not going to care what happens to her or whether she finds another home–they'd probably enjoy seeing her fall into a large mud puddle and the sooner the better!

Delete adverbs contentedly and heavily as they weigh down the narrative. Ditto rather and really.

Passive

"What a boring place the cow paddock was, she thought. Nothing ever happened–it was boring. She didn't want to live here anymore."

This is passive. **Active** is always more interesting and immediate:

"What a boring place the cow paddock is. Nothing ever happens. It's boring. I don't want to live here anymore."

No need for she thought following What a boring place the cow paddock is as the sentence is Jossie's thoughts.

Stating that Jossie hadn't thought yet, and making her sigh heavily, shows she hasn't given any serious thought to her idea of moving and is still at the moaning-mini stage.

Condense that waffle to two sentences that introduce the protagonist, state her problem and how she intends to solve it.

Jossie the Jersey cow was tired of living in a paddock.
So she went looking for a new home.

The Wrong Central Character

Be careful not to choose the **wrong central character**. In the above excerpt, the other cow sounds more interesting–the wrong central character.

If you find one of your other characters seems stronger and wants to take over, then perhaps the story is about that character.

Check your plot and character arc thoroughly to make sure you've chosen the **right** central character.

Pitfalls to be Aware of in the Middle

Again, it's easy to become bogged down in the middle of your story and lose your way with overwriting, over explanation or weighty narrative in the imagined belief you need to include every dramatic scene you have ever heard of.

If you've plotted your character arc correctly and know where your character is headed, don't deviate from this planned path by adding extra scenes that might sound wonderfully entertaining yet add nothing to the story and might even be distracting.

Stay true to your protagonist's adventure. This is their story; not a list of dramatic, overblown, unconnected events.

The Shrimp Who Wanted to be Pink

Two children were at the beach, building a sandcastle.
The little shrimp swam up close to them. And because he was semi-transparent the children couldn't see him and scooped him up in a brilliant-yellow plastic bucket.

There's no need to describe the children–neither is the central character. A brief explanation of them building a sandcastle is sufficient.

Stay with the main protagonist; the little shrimp and his obsession with the colour pink. This is his story and his adventure.

The Wrong Central Characters

Don't be persuaded to add more details about the children. It might be something like this:

"I've never caught a shrimp before," said Jenny. "Look! It's quite a big shrimp, too!"

"Yes!" Billy exclaimed. "Let's put him in this pool we've made in the sand and see if we can catch another one."

This is now a story about the children–the wrong central characters. The little shrimp literally fades out of the picture.

Always stay with your main character and their problem/s.

Point of View - POV

Keep to the main protagonist's POV, in this instance the little shrimp. Allow him the last word/thought.

The little shrimp was surprised but not frightened. He swam round and round in the bucket. Brilliant yellow was a colourful colour too. But he still thought pink was better.

The children looked into the bucket. "Hey! We've caught a shrimp."

"Let's show Dad," they cried.

The little shrimp was quite happy to go with the children.

Pitfalls to Be Aware of at the End

Be wary of endings that tail off lamely or end abruptly without concise interpretation of both climax and resolution. Don't end your story because you've run out of steam, or reached your word limit, or because you're sick of your story and think it's time to end.

Make sure you explain everything and answer every question pertaining to theme, character arc, and storyline.

Your climax–whether it's a dramatic fight scene, a light bulb moment, or a slow realisation–needs to fit your protagonist's nature, and all that has gone before in the story. Don't have your protagonist engage in a battle if you haven't been leading up to a battle scene throughout the story. Similarly, don't give them a light bulb moment that has nothing to do with the story.

Stay true to your protagonist's chosen path. The decision they make to solve their problem needs to be the right one for them.

The Wrong Way

The Shrimp Who Wanted to be Pink

I hope those children fall over and drop the bucket near the sea so I can escape, thought the little shrimp sulkily. He sat in the yellow plastic bucket and cried colourless salty tears. "Oh, woe is me!"

Wrong! The little shrimp is now a sulky pain in the butt. He doesn't appear prepared to do anything to try and escape. His only hope of escape is if the children fall over and drop the bucket. No hero should act this way. He is reduced to moaning and crying.

The story has not reached the transition stage where the protagonist must make a decision and act on that decision.

Sebastian's Tail

The rat looked at Sebastian. "What sort of tail do you want?"

"It's no good." Sebastian sighed again. "I've tried all kinds of tails and none of them are any good. I'll just have to go throughout my life with no tail at all." He began to cry. "I don't want to try any more tails. They don't work!"

Wrong! Sebastian is fast becoming a moaning-mini. He's tried a few tails, they didn't work, and now he has given up.

No hero gives up, ever!

It might appear the story has reached a transition stage–with the hero giving up–but the only revelation is that Sebastian doesn't have any gumption.

The story deflates at this point and the reader is left feeling let down by a hero who won't get off his butt to help himself.

The Wrong Way to End Your Story

Having an angel/fairy/wizard float into the glade proudly carrying the perfect tail for Sebastian on a purple satin cushion patterned with gold stars is not the way to lift this story out of the doldrums.

Don't ever use this kind of solution for your hero. Not only are you introducing a character who has nothing to do with the story, you are allowing someone else–possibly an adult–to solve the protagonist's problem.

The **protagonist**, in this case, Sebastian, needs to find a solution to his problem.

Jossie's New Home

I've tried every place on this *#%! farm, and they all suck! Jossie stamped her hoof and glared out at the farm. Where to now? Her mouth drooped sourly. With a bad-tempered "moo!" she stalked back to the cow paddock, kicking out at a small rabbit sheltering behind a thistle.

Wow! There are so many mistakes here it's difficult to know where to begin.

An Unsympathetic Character

Jossie is now what is known an **unsympathetic character**. She is so bad-tempered, sulky and downright nasty no reader is going to care what happens to her. Indeed, they probably care more about the little rabbit sheltering behind a thistle.

Jossie has made no attempt to solve her problem, only complain and sulk and "kick out at the world," blaming everyone else for her problem.

No heroine ever behaves in this manner.

Exercise Eleven

1. Check your story thoroughly to make sure you haven't fallen into any of the above pitfalls.
2. Is your protagonist a sympathetic character?
3. Have you chosen the right central character?
4. Is your protagonist someone you'd like to know?

Chapter Nine

A Complete Story

I have yet to publish this children's picture book so the title is a working title only.

A Seashore Study

Our year four class went on a seashore study for our environmental project; and we got a shock.

At the beach, a man held up a dead seagull. He told us he was a scientist who studied birds.
"You're an ornithologist," said Damien, who always knew everything.
"That's right," said the man. "My name is Doctor Neilson."
Mrs Bruce, our teacher, looked pleased with Damien. She was always pleased with Damien.
"What happened to the bird?" Elsie looked like she might cry. Elsie cried at everything.
"It died," said Doctor Neilson. "And it's my job to find out why."
He placed the seagull on a wooden board. We crowded round as he took several instruments from his black bag.
"An operation," said Deepak who wanted to be a doctor when he grew up.
"A dissection," Damien emphasised, looking at Mrs Bruce.
"Don't crowd Doctor Neilson," said Mrs Bruce looking even more pleased with Damien.

We moved back a step as Doctor Neilson picked up a scalpel and cut into the dead bird.

"Yuck! Guts!" Charlie pulled a face. Charlie was always pulling faces.

Elsie started to cry.

"*Intestines*, Charlie." Mrs Bruce was not pleased with Charlie. "Stop crying, please, Elsie."

"I'm going to examine the bird's stomach contents," explained Doctor Neilson as he worked. "That might tell us why it died."

"Pooh!" Charlie held his nose.

"I'm going to be sick," said Teresa.

Mrs Bruce frowned at Charlie and said, "Move away, please, Teresa, if you're going to be sick."

"Now, can anyone tell me what they see?" Doctor Neilson spread smelly stuff on the wooden board.

"Rubbish and intestines!" shouted Charlie, making gagging noises.

We all laughed, except Elsie and Teresa.

"Very observant, Charlie," said Mrs Bruce.

"An accurate observation," smiled Doctor Neilson.

Charlie looked pleased with himself.

"Not accurate enough," muttered Damien.

"What's this?" Doctor Neilson held up a length of thin coiled line.

"Fishing line," I said before Damien could say it.

"*Nylon* fishing line, Ella," said Damien.

I pretended not to hear him.

"Correct," said Doctor Neilson. "And this?"

"Part of a bottle top," said Teresa, forgetting about being sick.

"And this?"

"A red bead," said Kerry. Kerry collected beads.

"Children, make a list of everything we identify," said Mrs Bruce.

We got out our pencils and notebooks. Inside the bird's stomach were tiny bits of fabric, plastic and polystyrene chips, part of a silver can tab and the tip of a striped drinking straw.

"Is that why the bird died?" asked Deepak.

"Yes." Doctor Neilson nodded. "All this litter is toxic to the bird and has poisoned it. And see how full its stomach was? There's no room for food."

By now none of us were laughing. Not even Charlie.

"Will other birds die, too?" Elsie looked like she might cry again.

"Many more." Doctor Neilson packed his instruments into his black bag and placed the bird and the stomach contents into separate plastic bags.

We sat on the beach and ate our lunch. No one talked much because we were thinking about the birds that would die. There were plenty flying around. Several gathered at our feet. Mrs Bruce said we were not to feed them crusts.

"It's not their natural food." Damien sounded as superior as ever.

Mrs Bruce gave Damien a small smile and asked Charlie to collect our food scraps. When he'd finished, he didn't have to be told to take the plastic bag to the rubbish bin.

We searched the beach for litter. It was amazing what we found; a whole plastic bag full! Charlie carried the plastic bag to the rubbish bin.

Then the bus arrived to take us back to school.

We made a giant poster of the beach for our environmental project. Everyone had space in the poster to draw what they liked. Charlie drew intestines. Elsie drew the dead seagull. Damien drew Doctor Neilson dissecting the seagull. Deepak drew Doctor's Neilson's black bag. Teresa drew lots of bottle tops and Kerry drew beads.

I drew seagulls flying and sitting on the beach.

We helped Mrs Bruce tack the poster to the classroom wall and stood back to admire our work. I thought Mrs Bruce looked a bit sad. And then Charlie walked over to the poster and wrote along the bottom in big red letters:

Don't be a litterbug! Litter goes in the bin not on the beach.

We all clapped. Even Damien. Mrs Bruce looked very pleased with Charlie.

My Idea

My **idea** for the story arose from an environmental aspect: the consequences of rubbish in our oceans. I've made mention of my love of the sea and beaches, so the subject is dear to my heart.

Every time I walk the beach, I pick up rubbish; mostly plastics but also a wide variety of other items. It depends on which way the wind is blowing; if it's from the east, there's more rubbish.

N.B. You never know when your observations of "the weather" might be useful to include in your stories.

A List

And so I began my **list**: plastic bags, drinking straws, balloons, bottles, lids, beads, pegs, toys, hard plastics, bottle tops, fishing line, pieces of fabric, food, polystyrene chips, cans, silver can tabs, cigarette butts, sea, waves, beach, seagulls, sunshine, blue sky, wind, sand, children, laughter, chatter, schoolbags, teacher, scientist, intestines, board, knife, black bag, utensils, books, pens, pencils, lunch, sandwiches, food scraps, classroom, bus, school, poster, etc.

Building Setting, Characters and Atmosphere

As I mentioned previously, it doesn't matter if you don't use everything on your list; you are building your **setting**, **characters** and **atmosphere**.

Characters

Next, I had to think of my characters and establish my main protagonist/s. As I mentioned in an earlier chapter, I tend to make things up as I write. Charlie grew on me throughout the story until he became one of the main protagonists. He's the comic of the bunch; there's always one. Charlie risks the wrath of the teacher by shouting out observations, making gagging noises, acting the clown, etc.

Ella narrates the story, so she is the main protagonist. We experience everything through her eyes:

1. The interaction, byplay and classroom rivalry between the children.
2. Ella's annoyance at Damien who always knew everything.
3. Ella's sympathy–or perhaps disdain–for Else who cried at everything.
4. Ella's amusement at Charlie's antics.
5. Ella's shock at the reason the bird died.
6. Ella's awakening awareness of her surroundings–more birds might die.
7. Ella's admiration and pleasure at making the poster.
8. Ella noticing that Mrs Bruce looked a bit sad.
9. Ella's approval that Mrs Bruce is finally very pleased with Charlie.

The Beginning: Who, What, Where, When, Why

Remember, the **beginning** introduces the **protagonist/s** and outlines any **problems** they might encounter.

1. Who? The children–our year four class.
2. What? Went on a seashore study.
3. Where? The beach.
4. When? Morning.
5. Why? To find ideas for our environmental project.

The "why?" is where you find your **theme** and the protagonist's **internal problem**. The children explore the seashore for their environmental project, but we always need to delve deeper by asking, "Why do they do this?" or "What will they learn/discover about the world/themselves through this adventure?"

Ella's announcement at the end of the opening sentence; and we got a shock, leads the reader into the story and to muse, "I wonder what happened?"

Without Ella's announcement the opening sentence sounds rather flat; the reader might think, "So what?" or "Who cares?"

If the opening sentence in *Sebastian's Tail* was; Sebastian the rat was born without a tail, the reader would be left thinking, "Oh, poor thing," or "How sad." There would be nothing to draw the reader into the story or wonder, "What happened?" Although, they might wonder, "Why was he born without a tail? But it's not enough. The extra sentence; So he set out to find one, is needed to let the reader know what the story will be about.

Ella's announcement; and we got a shock, is needed in *A Seashore Study* to lead the reader into the story.

Themes

You should never try to "thrash your theme at every turn," thereby, putting off your readers or pulling them out of the story.

You don't want your reader noticing how many times you represent your theme, e.g. "how water affects our lives," by referencing the necessity of water to sustain the lives of all living things at every turn with mention of rivers, lakes, the ocean, piped water in the city, lack of water in the desert, etc. Your reader will start noticing every reference to water, become annoyed, forget about your story and toss your book aside.

To avoid this happening, it's wise to present several themes.

Keep it subtle and always let the story speak for itself.

In *A Seashore Study*, the most obvious theme is the environmental one: the consequences of rubbish in our oceans.

The children are working on their environmental project, so they have obviously studied environmental issues–both in the classroom and possibly for homework as well–before setting out for the beach. Doctor Neilson takes their studies to the next level with his dissection of the bird.

The children are made aware of what is happening in the world around them, even on a beach, a place normally associated with fun. They are confronted with life and death/loss of innocence.

We sat on the beach and ate our lunch. No one talked much because we were thinking about the birds that would die.

There are other themes at work here, too. Can you find them?

Have another look through the list of the narrator, Ella's, thoughts.

Growth of Protagonist/s

Your protagonist/s need to grow throughout the story. They must learn something from their adventures and emerge better for the experience; their **internal journey**.

"It's not their natural food." Damien sounded as superior as ever.

Mrs Bruce gave Damien a small smile and asked Charlie to collect our food scraps. When he'd finished, he didn't have to be told to take the plastic bag to the rubbish bin.

Damien

Damien's superiority draws only a slight smile from Mrs Bruce. Is she growing tired of Damien?

Always leave something for your reader to discover and to acknowledge, to nod their head wisely over and say, "Yes, I know children like (Damien)."

We are all different and have annoying habits/traits. We're human. Always make your characters human with their faults and their strengths. No one is perfect.

Damien redeems himself at the end of the story by applauding Charlie's actions.

Charlie

Mrs Bruce asks Charlie to collect the food scraps. Charlie doesn't need to be told to take the plastic bag to the rubbish bin. He has stopped clowning around and has begun to notice what is happening in the world around him, to take charge, to grow up.

And then Charlie walked over to the poster and wrote along the bottom in big red letters;

"Don't be a litterbug! Litter goes in the bin not on the beach."

We all clapped. Even Damien. Mrs Bruce looked very pleased with Charlie.

Charlie has "stepped up to the mark" proved himself to be resourceful and finally won the approval of Mrs Bruce and all his classmates. He has emerged a winner; he has come of age.

The Children as a Group

The last scene also presents the children as a united group. They have worked hard on their environmental poster, reached an understanding/acceptance of their world, and are pleased with their efforts; they have come of age.

I think Mrs Bruce has also learned something about herself, her students and life itself, don't you?

Protagonist's Problem and Internal Journey

If your protagonist doesn't appear to change/grow throughout your story, go back over your manuscript and check that you have presented your protagonist's problem/s with clarity.

If the protagonist's internal journey is not as clear or as deep as you need it to be, search for a place where you can present a problem for your protagonist to solve; one that allows them to learn something about themselves and the wider world. Remember, it must fit in with your theme/s and story; it can't be an unconnected event.

You Don't Have to Explain Everything

You don't always have to explain everything down to the last tiny detail. Always leave something for your reader; hidden subtleties your reader will enjoy uncovering.

Sometimes, it's what you don't say; something that makes them smile in appreciation and say, "Ah, I know exactly what the author means."

We have analysed several children's picture books in this section. Let's look again at the seven basic plots and see if we can work out the plots for the stories we studied. See if you can pick the plot for *The Three Billy Goats Gruff*.

The Seven Basic Plots-Wikipedia

1. Overcoming the Monster
2. Rags to Riches
3. The Quest
4. Voyage and Return
5. Comedy
6. Tragedy
7. Rebirth

Jossie's New Home–the quest.
Jamie's Monsters–overcoming the monster.
Sebastian's Tail–the quest.
One Haunted House–overcoming the monster.
The Shrimp Who Wanted to be Pink–the quest.
A Seashore Study –the quest.

Plots

The quest was the plot in four stories: *Jossie's New Home, Sebastian's Tail, The Shrimp Who Wanted to be Pink* and *A Seashore Study*. Although the four stories share the same plot, the sub-plots, characters, settings, themes, tone, pace, and nuances are entirely different for each story.

Overcoming the monster, the plot in *Jamie's Monsters* and *One Haunted House* again, presents two entirely different stories with different characters, settings, themes, etc.

Never worry about presenting the same plot, over and over again; there are, after all, only seven basic plots.

It's what your characters do, how they act/react to their surroundings and challenges that make your stories unique.

Writing Children's Picture Books

Writing children's picture books can indeed be challenging; but the reward for producing a book that children, parents and teachers admire is well worth taking up that challenge.

Be patient.

Write with honesty and sincerity and you will succeed.

Good Luck!

Chapter Ten

Publishing, Marketing, Selling

You've written your children's picture book. What's next?
There are several options:

1. You can send your manuscript to a publisher or an agent.
2. You can self-publish.

Illustrations

To be accepted by publishers, the manuscript must work without illustrations. If it doesn't and you need to write a four-page letter explaining your story, then it's not likely your manuscript will be accepted.

That doesn't mean you have to put every tiny detail into your manuscript in an attempt to help the editor understand the story; far from it. Keep your sentences and paragraphs short and to the point.

Let the story speak for itself.

Publishers

Most publishers have different requirements for manuscripts which can be found on their websites. Do your research. Don't send picture books to publishers who only publish fantasy novels or non-fiction.

Study the books published by your chosen publishing company. Will your book fit the publisher's lists?

Don't waste their time and yours by sending your manuscript to the wrong publishing company.

Cover Letters

1. Keep your cover letter short and to the point, one page at most; editors are busy people.
2. The standard regulation is to send in the manuscript only without illustrations. Most publishers have their own field of illustrators.
3. Don't include instructions on how you wish your book to look, or suggestions for illustrations.
4. Include a concise synopsis of your story, and a short biography detailing your writing/publishing experience; keep this to a paragraph or two.
5. Be polite, professional and patient.
6. Don't phone or write asking if they received your manuscript. Wait for them to contact you.

First-time authors of a children's picture book can enter the Joy Cowley Award (New Zealand) or other competitions for unpublished writers where the winning manuscript is published by a reputable publisher. Always check competition rules. Generally, you can't send your manuscript to another publisher while the competition is running, so note this ties up your manuscript for a certain time span.

The world of publishing is continually changing; you will need to keep up with the latest trends.

Self-Publishing

If you wish to self-publish your children's picture book, there are several options. All require research and thought.

Publishing Sites

You can self-publish through Amazon.com; a physical book through CreateSpace and an eBook through Kindle Direct Publishing (KDP). Each site has videos and instructions to show you how to do this. If you're new to this procedure, remember it will take time to learn each step. Ask for help. They have a team of people who have always been very helpful to me.

NB. The world of digital publishing is constantly changing, and even as I write this CreateSpace and KDP are merging. KDP will now publish both paperbacks and eBooks.

Other publishing sites are: Kobo, IngramSpark, Smashwords and Draft2Digital. You can publish your book to every site but you need to understand what each site's requirements are regarding ISBN numbers, cover measurements, interior book formatting, pricing, etc. The key is research. All sites are continually changing/updating.

If you don't want to design and format your book yourself, you can pay someone to do this for you. They will also load (publish) the book to different sites.

Costs involved include paying for an editor–highly recommended– illustrations and a cover. Again, research is required to find cover designers, graphic designers, illustrators, editors and formatters. Try fiverr.com and other internet sites that provide the people you need.

You can advertise for an illustrator, graphic designer, editor and formatter on Facebook and other social media sites.

Read other author's stories of how they published their books; be aware of pitfalls and possibilities. Don't rush ahead with the first offer; always consider at least three different proposals.

This can run into money; be aware of every aspect before you begin.

Printing: Off-Set, Digital and POD (Print on Demand)

You can choose either a digital or an off-set printing company to print your children's picture books. Most countries offer this option. Again, check prices from at least three different printers before you decide as you will need to consider the cost of higher print runs versus cost of lower print runs. Most off-set printing companies usually require you to order 1,000 copies or more. The higher the print run, the lower the cost per book.

There are smaller print runs offered by different companies—mostly digital—but at a higher cost per book. It depends on how many copies you want.

You can order as many POD books as you want from KDP, Smashwords, etc.

My children's picture books were printed by an off-set printer in New Zealand, although I do have one children's picture book with KDP.

Selling

Libraries order books through different companies who specialize in this service. Again, research is the key. Libraries may also buy from on-line stores, and may buy directly from the author; it depends where you live.

The business of selling books is constantly changing, especially with the event of self-publishing. Many authors sell from their websites, or sites like Amazon, ebay or Etsy.

Try your local schools, childcare centres and kindergartens, book stores and craft markets.

I sell my children's picture books at craft markets, to libraries, schools, childcare centres and kindergartens, as well as online.

Non-Fiction

If you don't want to write fiction, writing non-fiction might appeal. Research your topic of choice before you begin to determine what has already been written about the subject.

What special knowledge do you have? Is it a suitable subject for a children's non-fiction picture book? Do you know of someone with knowledge and experience on a topic you wish to write about. Most people are happy to help a writer with subject matter and don't mind answering questions and sharing their experiences.

It goes without saying to always be polite and treat them with respect and thank them for their help and advice.

Exercise Twelve

1. Examine your special knowledge of a subject or subjects and decide if you want to write fiction or non-fiction.
2. Research your subject.
3. Make notes and lists.
4. Try your hand at writing a cover letter.

Chapter Eleven

Short Stories

Writing for older children is both challenging and rewarding. The books are longer, so you have room for deeper character development, plot, setting, etc.

Greater description is needed unless the story is accompanied by black-and-white drawings–often found in chapter books, short stories and graphic novels.

Longer books rely mostly on cover design for physical representation of characters and setting.

That stated, a lot can be said in a few words.

Let's look first at one of my short stories *Nothing to Do* which was produced on National Radio, New Zealand 1993

Author's Note: A bach is a small holiday home in New Zealand. In the North Island we call our holiday homes baches. In the South Island they are called cribs.

Nothing to Do

"What a dump!" Brett stared up and down the deserted road, with its rows of equally deserted waterfront baches. "How do live here?" He kicked at a stone. "There's nothing to do."

David frowned round at the small bay where he lived. Last night's heavy rain had filled the creek with muddy water. Fishing was out.

"Bet they don't have any spacies?" Brett thrust his hands into the pockets of his designer jeans.

"Round at the shop." David picked up a stone and threw it into the muddy water.

"Yeah?" For the first time since his arrival the previous evening, Brett's sullen expression cleared. "Let's go." He started off in the direction of the car.

"We have to walk." David threw another stone. He was getting sick of Brett.

"Walk?" Brett stopped. "What can't your mother drive us?"

"Mum needs the car." David's expression didn't change. "It's only round the road."

"It's going to rain." Brett gestured up at the grey winter sky.

"We'll take out coats." David turned back to the house.

Brett followed, muttering, "Some holiday."

David didn't say much as they walked the one kilometre to the shop. He didn't feel like showing Brett any of his secret haunts. And he doubted if Brett would think it any fun to sneak into old Baker's property and pinch oranges.

Brett kept up a continuous stream of complaints about the winding road, the cold, the "dead mud" that passed for a beach and how he didn't want to get his new Reeboks dirty.

David was glad when they reached the shop. He only had a dollar, but Brett pulled out a twenty dollar note. They got some change and went round to the video parlour next door.

"Is this it?" Brett's lip curled as he looked at the dingy little room with its concrete floor and the two video games along one wall.

David didn't answer. At least there were only two other boys playing the spacies. He nodded to the two boys, then leant against the wall and watched them hitting the control buttons. Lights flashed and the spacies hummed.

Brett sauntered over to one of the boys. "Give you five bucks if you let me have the spacie." He held out a five dollar note.

After a surprised stare, the boy let go of the controls. "You're on!" He reached for the note and pocketed it. "Want the other one, too?" He nodded across at his friend, who had also stopped playing his video game.

Without a word, Brett handed across another five dollar bill.

The two boys went gleefully from the room rolling their eyes and making faces at David as they went out through the door.

David had watched all this in disbelief. Now he went over to Brett.

"What did you do that for?"

"I wanted the spacies." Brett slotted in a twenty cent coin and began bashing at the controls. "You can play that one." He nodded carelessly across at the other video game.

"No thanks," David muttered and turned for the door. Outside he kicked at a stone and deliberately splashed through a puddle. He hadn't been this mad in a long time. He could hear the spacies singing, but the sound had lost all appeal.

The other two boys saw him and came running up. They were licking huge ice-creams.

"Hey, David. Who's your friend?"

"Yeah, what a geek." They both laughed and went strolling off toward the football field.

"Give you five bucks for a lick of your ice-cream," David heard one of them say.

His face red, he set off in the opposite direction. When he reached the little bridge, he leant on it and stared down into the water. How was he going to put up with Brett for a whole week? Especially if the weather kept up. For the first time in his life, David felt dissatisfied with his home. Brett was right. It was a dump. He was embarrassed by that dingy video parlour.

Loud laughter came from the football field. Other children surrounded the two boys. They were all looking over at David, pointing and laughing.

David looked back down at the muddy river. Even his friends were laughing at him. He picked up a stone and tossed it into the swirling waters. He was so engrossed in his thoughts he didn't notice Brett walking towards him.

"Stupid spacies." Brett kicked at the concrete bridge railing.

For the first time in hours, David felt like smiling. Both video games were tricky to operate. You had to know exactly when to push the controls. Especially Galaxia. But he wasn't going to tell Brett.

"Want to go back, then?" he asked.

Brett said nothing. He looked as sullen as the gathering rain clouds. On the way back they got caught in a shower of rain and had to shelter beneath trees.

At the house, Brett flopped in front of the television. David went into the garage to sort out the fishing lines. He'd been going to do it for months.

About half-an-hour later, Brett wandered out. "What are you doing?" he asked.

"Sorting out my lines." David didn't look up.

"Dad's got a launch and we go fishing a lot. Out in the gulf."

Brett sounded and looked so superior that David could have kicked him. "I'm going to get pipis," he said. "Perhaps a few paddle crabs." He looked at Brett's designer jeans and white Reeboks. "You wouldn't want to come. You've got to be quick to catch paddle crabs. They bite." He didn't bother hiding the scorn he felt, even though his mother had told him not to be rude.

"I'm quick." Brett straightened away from the door. "Bet I could catch one."

David shrugged. He took of his old shoes and dragged on his gumboots. Then he picked up a bucket and headed for the door. Brett grabbed another bucket and trailed after him.

David stopped. "If you're coming, you'd better wear the spare gumboots." He waited for Brett to refuse. Brett never took off his Reeboks.

Brett hesitated briefly, then took off his Reeboks and pulled on the gumboots. They were covered in mud, but he didn't say anything.

David didn't speak either as they went out to the main road and crossed over to the beach. If Brett started complaining, he'd ignore him. He set off across the mud-flats, deliberately choosing the boggiest patches of mud to wade through.

When they reached the creek, he stopped. He knew the creek was only ankle deep, but the muddy water made it look deeper. "Do you want to go back?" he asked Brett.

Brett frowned down at the creek then over at the mud on the other side. "Nah. Might as well carry on, now that I'm here." He shrugged and pretended to look bored.

They splashed their way across to the other side and through the mud. It stank, but Brett never said a word.

"Look! The shag's got a fish." David pointed upwards.

"Where?" Brett stumbled to a stop beside him.

They watched the shag fly above them, a small fish dangling from its bill.

"Where are the pipis and paddle crabs?" Brett demanded.

"Over on the sand bank." David pointed to where the river joined the open sea.

They walked on, crunching their way over mounds of broken pipi shells. Oyster catchers scolded their progress. David stopped to take a deep breath. He loved the smell of the sea. He noticed, in amusement, that Brett copied him.

Other people were at the sandbanks, heads down, bottoms up, digging for pipis. David waded into the water, squatted down, and started to dig.

"How do you know where to dig?" Brett stood at the water's edge.

"You have to dig about until you find one. They're usually in a group of about five," David explained. "Here's one." He held up a big pipi, its white shell edged in black.

Brett waded gingerly into the water and even more gingerly, dug about in the sand.

"I've got one!" He held it up in triumph.

"Put it in the bucket," David told him, remembering back to the first time he'd found a pipi. It took the boys a while to get half a bucket full. David had almost forgotten about paddle crabs, when Brett let out a yell.

"A paddle crab!" David shouted. "Quick, it's getting away." He groped after the crab. He might have known Brett would be useless.

"I see it." Brett splashed after the crab.

"Where?" David followed.

"Thought I saw a leg. There!" Brett plunged his arm into the water and pulled up the crab by one of its legs. He let it go with another yell. The crab hit the water with a "plop!"

David grabbed it by its back. "You've got to hold it by its back. See?" He showed Brett. "Then it can't bite you." The crab waved its large claws about but it couldn't reach David's fingers.

"I'll put it back in the bucket and you can try picking it up," he told Brett.

He put the crab into the bucket where it sat waving its claws menacingly up at the two boys.

After a moment Brett make a quick grab and picked it up. "Got it!" He held it up to David. They examined the crab a while longer, then Brett put it back into the bucket.

They caught two more paddle crabs then David announced it was time to go.

"Do we have to?" Brett looked up from his pile of sand.

"Yeah. The tide's coming in. We can come back tomorrow." He let Brett carry the bucket with the paddle crabs.

They were halfway back when David saw a group of children racing up and down the beach. He recognized the two boys from the video parlour. Once, he would have run over to join in. But not today. He hoped they wouldn't see him and Brett. It was a hopeless thought. They were soon spotted and the two boys came running over. When they saw who it was with David, they smirked.

"What did you get?" They tried to see into the bucket.

Brett put the bucket down and picked up a paddle crab. The way David had shown him. "A paddle crab," He held it up. The two boys leapt back.

"Good size crab," David said.

"Not bad," one of the boys acknowledged.

"We got two others and some pipis." Brett held out the bucket as if he'd been catching paddle crabs all his life.

David looked at Brett. His hair had been messed up by the wind, mud clung to his clothes and the designer jeans were soaked. But his eyes were shinning as brightly as the afternoon sunshine that had chased away the morning's rain.

As he followed the others back to the beach, David looked up at the sky. Brett hadn't turned out too bad. If it was fine tomorrow they might even go fishing.

Chapter Twelve

Putting Together *Nothing to Do*

I wrote this story a few years ago now, and it was produced on National Radio as I mentioned above. Stories for radio need to be of a certain length to fit time slots, usually fifteen minutes. Always check the word length required. Read your story out loud to see if it fits this time slot.

The Beginning

Once again, the **beginning** introduces the **main characters**, and poses the **protagonist**, David's, **problem**/challenge; how will he cope with Brett? This is the story character arc and won't be resolved until the end. Other problems arise throughout the story–peaks/grey spots–but are resolved at the time and don't detract from the major problem.

Brett's accusations, What a dump! How do you live here? and There's nothing to do, sum up what he thinks of both David and David's home, and presents perhaps the greatest fears facing children on holiday; that they might be bored or their holiday ruined. Brett followed muttering, "Some holiday."

Fishing was out, highlights David's reaction to Brett's remarks–not only is fishing out, but so is everything else.

He didn't feel like showing Brett any of his secret haunts.

1. Set up a battlefield for your characters to "thrash things out."
2. David's **external** problem is; how will he cope with Brett?
3. His **internal** problem is; will they find friendship?

The Middle

As we move though the story, the middle, David is forced to see his home through Brett's eyes; the winding road, the dead mud that passed for a beach, the dingy video parlour. For the first time in his life David is dissatisfied with his home, even dissatisfied with his life, and this makes him dislike Brett even more. When Brett embarrasses him in front of his friends by buying the video machines, and then offering one to David, he refuses the offer, Brett and everything Brett stands for.

He hadn't been this mad in a long time.

David wonders how he will put up with Brett for a whole week.
David's major problem is compounded by each annoying thing Brett does.
When his friends laugh at him and call Brett a geek–thereby making David a geek, too, by association–David sets off in the opposite direction from his friends, from Brett, from the things that have embarrassed and angered him. He doesn't feel comfortable anywhere anymore and wanders about in no-man's-land for a while before finally making a stand of sorts on the little bridge (his castle) where he tosses a stone into the swirling muddy waters. His life at the moment is muddy, he can't face his friends, and his holiday is ruined by Brett.
The first ray of sunshine for David is when Brett fails to work the video machines.

For the first time in hours David felt like smiling.
(A peak/grey spot).

His amusement is only temporary; there's still the rest of the week to get through. Back at the house David goes to sort out his fishing lines. He tries to sort out the problem of Brett–David's external problem. Brett comes to investigate, still superior in his designer jeans and boasting of his Dad's launch. David has finally had enough of Brett and even though his mother had told him not to be rude, issues his challenge:

"You wouldn't want to come. You've got to be quick to catch paddle crabs. They bite."

Brett bites back:

"I'm quick. Bet I could catch one."

He's ready to accept David's challenge–perhaps he wants to be friends after all?
David's not convinced and waits for Brett to take off his Reeboks. Brett never took off his Reeboks–his armour against the dump. The first thawing in the relationship is when Brett does take off his Reeboks and accepts the spare pair of gumboots even though they were covered in mud, without complaining.
David is still putting Brett through his paces though, by not talking, and deliberately choosing the boggiest patches of mud to wade through. When they reach the creek–the line drawn in the sand–he waits to see if Brett will cross over and continue with their adventure or return to the sulks. Brett's ungracious, "Might as well carry on, now that I'm here," is enough to earn him a small reward from David who points out the shag with the fish. Brett looks, but still demands to know where the pipis and crabs are.

They crunch onwards; things are still rocky in their relationship. But when David stops to take a deep breath–a pause in their adventure/relationship–Brett copies him, which suggests Brett is warming to their adventure/friendship.

But when they reach the pipi bed, Brett is still a fish out of water and is forced to ask David, "How do you know where to dig?" David shows Brett how to find the pipis, and when Brett finally finds one, David is able to share Brett's triumph, albeit wryly, by remembering back to when he'd first found a pipi. He offers the olive branch;

"Put it in the bucket."

The End

The climax of the story is the arrival of the paddle crab–the final challenge for both boys. David's first thought is: He might have known Brett would be useless. But he's forced to undergo a change of mind when Brett makes an attempt to catch the crab. Impressed that Brett has had a go–perhaps he's not so useless after all–David shows him how to catch the crab and hold it so that it doesn't bite. "See?" he tells Brett. He wants Brett to see not only the crab, but other things as well, like how great it is here in the bay, his home.

Brett has another go and is successful. The boys examine the crab together, the first thing they have accomplished together.

Now the two boys can share the experience of catching paddle crabs, digging for pipis, finding friendship, and enjoying their holiday together.

But there's still the problem of David's other friends to resolve.

"They were halfway back when David saw a group of children."

David and Brett are only halfway into their friendship. There are still things to be sorted.

Brett rises to the other boys' challenge, "What have you got?" by showing them the paddle crab, holding it the way David had shown him. The other boys acknowledge the good size crab, Brett's accomplishment, Brett himself, and David's friendship with Brett.

"They leapt back."

The Resolution

The story ends with David noticing that Brett's hair had been messed up by the wind, mud clung to his clothes and the designer jeans were soaked.

Brett has undergone his "trial by mud" and passed the test.

David acknowledges that Brett hadn't turned out too bad, and that "they might even go fishing the next day." He is now happy to show Brett some of his favourite haunts, to acknowledge him as his friend. His internal problem has been solved.

The theme is friendship. The story could also be called a coming-of-age story.

The Idea

My idea for the story arose from a question I posed; what would happen if a town boy came to stay with a country boy for the school holidays? This got me to thinking of the differences in their backgrounds: family, living conditions, familiar objects, interaction with others, hobbies, usual haunts, etc. The questions I kept asking myself needed answers; eventually, I had the basis of my story.

Then I needed a setting.

Building a Setting for Your Characters

To build my setting for *Nothing to Do*, I thought of the places the boys were likely to visit or explore during their time together, and the things they might encounter: beach, rocks, river, sea, pipis, paddle crab, shag, shells, mud, bridge, road, fishing rods, bucket, shoes, gumboots, hats, other children, video parlour, shop, ice cream, etc.

I lived at a small bay for several years, so I used the bay, the surrounds and my experiences of living there as my setting. Yes, this does include digging for pipis and catching paddle crabs! My son and I often walked out at low tide to the pipi bed to get pipis for our dinner or to use as bait when we went fishing.

Writing of the familiar will always lend your stories authenticity and colour.

Planning

I don't plan out the whole story before I begin; I usually begin with an idea and see where the story leads me. Even though Brett is not the main protagonist, I decided to begin with him; and to use dialogue to open the story. When Brett scorns the area, calling it a dump and asks, "How do you live here?" the reader knows he is speaking to the main protagonist even though he has yet to be introduced. And they can also sense the main protagonist's hackles rising at Brett's taunts.

To plan your short story:

1. Begin with an idea; your theme.
2. Develop your characters and character arc.
3. Build your setting/s.
4. Work out your plot/story line.

Rewriting a Classic Fairy Story

You might like to try your hand at rewriting a classic fairy story like *Cinderella, Sleeping Beauty, Hansel and Gretel, Rapunzel* or *Little Red Riding Hood.*

To achieve this you really need to turn the story upside down or write from a different viewpoint.

I have rewritten *Little Red Riding Hood* from the grandmother's POV.

Below is the story.

From the Inside

Where the devil was that chit of a girl, Red Riding Hood? The Grandmother tightened her knitted shawl around her shoulders and frowned. The youth of today cared little for the older generation. Here she was practically starving to death waiting for her granddaughter to arrive with her weekly basket of goodies and where was the girl? Dawdling, that's where!

Half an hour later, she heard the catch on the front door open. About time!

"Is that you, Red Riding Hood?" she called then nearly fell out of bed when a big grey wolf strode into the bedroom.

"No, it's not Red Riding Hood." The wolf smacked his chops. "But I did meet her... in the woods." He sidled closer. "I saw a huntsman, too. But I soon gave him the slip."

"You keep back, you great brute!" The grandmother reached for her walking stick. "What have you done with my granddaughter?"

"Nothing... yet." The wolf looked sly.

"Get out!" The grandmother lifted her stick.

The wolf brushed it aside, lunged for the bed and gobbled up the grandmother in one huge gulp.

Lord! It was dark and slimy in the wolf's stomach. It smelled, too, with flabby bits of goodness knows what poking into her at every turn as the wolf strolled around the room. He'd better not touch anything of hers! She heard the scrape of the wardrobe door. If he was after money, he was out of luck! She grimaced with discomfort as the wolf walked to and fro, muttering, "This shawl will do... and these glasses. There! I look just like the grandmother. Red Riding Hood won't know the difference."

Oh, won't she! The grandmother tightened her mouth. We'll see about that! My granddaughter is no slouch when it comes to disguises.

She felt the wolf give a huge leap and had to hang on tightly to a fleshy bit of the wolf's intestine. Her head banged against his awful ribcage then she was stretched out as the wolf lay down... in her bed? The nasty, unfeeling monster. Ugh! Her face pressed against the wolf's innards and she could hardly breathe. Bother! If she had her little nail scissors with her, she'd cut her way out in seconds!

Moments later the bedroom door opened.

"Good afternoon, Grandmother."

"No, no I'm in here!" The grandmother tried to yell, but no words came out.

"Come in, child," said the wolf.

The grandmother nearly laughed at the sound of his imitation Grandmother voice. He didn't sound a bit like her. Red Riding Hood wouldn't be fooled for a minute.

"Why... Grandmother? What big eyes you have!" Red Riding Hood sounded amazed, not frightened, and the grandmother held her breath as she listened.

"All the better with which to see you, my dear," said the wolf.

"Why... Grandmother? What big ears you have!"

"All the better with which to hear you, my dear," said the wolf.

"Why… Grandmother? What big teeth you have!"

"All the better with which to eat you, my dear!"

The grandmother's head hit the wolf's ribcage again as the wolf give another leap. There was the sound of scuffles and a scream then Red Riding Hood tumbled in on top of her.

"What? You couldn't see that wasn't me?" The grandmother scowled at her granddaughter.

"Why, Grandmother! The wolf has eaten us!"

"Don't get into a flap, child. We're not done yet. Hark!"

"What have we here!" a voice roared.

"It's the huntsman," said the grandmother. Her cheeks began to glow.

She heard a loud retort then the wolf was still. Moments later light shone in on them and hands were reaching in to lift them out of the wolf's stomach.

The grandmother stood beside the huntsman and looked up into his eyes.

"About time," she said.

The Short Story Genre

If the short story genre appeals to you why not have a go?

Remember, you can write about most subjects; fiction or non-fiction.

Try your hand at rewriting a fairy story if you wish.

Good luck!

Chapter Thirteen

Chapter Books

Chapter books are roughly 8-10,000 words in length and usually written for the seven to ten-year-old age group. Books might have black and white illustrations, others no illustrations. Either way is acceptable.

Obviously, with the greater word length, there's room for deeper character development, more characters, expansion of plot and sub-plots, and the opportunity to expand your setting.

Dialogue and Narrative

Approximately a **third** of the book should be **narrative**, a **third dialogue**, and a **third introspection**–protagonist's inner thoughts. This gives the story balance. Children, or for that matter, any reader, don't want to read pages and pages of boring narrative and introspection regarding what the main protagonist should do, might do, but didn't. They tend to skip over these pages until they come to the dialogue and something interesting. (Go on. Admit that's what you do, too!)

Keep your chapters short and of similar length so children can read a chapter at a single sitting.

Following, is the beginning of my chapter book, *The Giant Greglusam* Jupiter Publishing 2014/Judy Lawn 2018

Remember, the **beginning** introduces the **protagonist** and outlines his/her **problems**.

The Giant Greglusam

Something washed up on the beach.

Samuel and Greg found it early one morning on the last day of the school holidays.

"What is it?" Greg crouched on the sand for a closer look.

"Looks pretty weird." Samuel spun his hat brim to the back of his head and cautiously dropped down beside Greg. The thing was weird. Like nothing he'd seen before; bigger than a large garden pot and rounded and sort of lumpy looking with an outer dirty brown crust.

He couldn't stop a shiver.

If only he could lose this being scared of everything? Ever since the "bad time," months ago, when his world had changed forever, Samuel had been scared. He hadn't told anyone of his feelings, especially not his mother. She was scared, too. She spent all her time watching his baby sister, Jasmine. And the look on her face scared Samuel more than anything.

Now he was scared of some stupid lumpy thing on the beach.

External and Internal Problems

Often the **external** and **internal** problems are more noticeable in a longer story.

In *The Giant Greglusam*, the story will show how Samuel copes with the "weird thing"–the external problem, and the "bad time"–the internal problem.

Both are resolved at the end of the story.

There's no need to describe in pages and pages of minute detail Samuel's internal problem in the beginning of the story. A hint is more than enough. Ditto the external problem.

If only he could lose this being scared of everything? Ever since the "bad time," months ago, when his world had changed forever, Samuel had been scared. He hadn't told anyone of his feelings, especially not his mother. She was scared, too. She spent all her time watching his baby sister, Jasmine. And the look on her face scared Samuel more than anything.

Now he was scared of some stupid lumpy thing on the beach.

Obviously, at an appropriate point in the story, the internal problem will have to be revealed. In the meantime, concentrate on the external problem of how Samuel deals with the "weird thing."

"Smells funny." Greg screwed up his nose.

"Yeah." Samuel pulled a face. "Maybe it's fish puke?"

Both boys laughed, even though Samuel knew his was forced.

Then Greg stretched out a finger.

Samuel held his breath. He wanted to tell Greg to watch out in case the thing had a sting or something. He'd read about jellyfish that could kill a person in minutes, and maybe this had been washed here from Australia or one of the Pacific islands by the spring storm that had raged for the last three days and kept them inside. Not that the thing looked like a jellyfish. Still, he couldn't help edging back a bit.

"Feels hard on the outside but kind of crumbly, too, and a bit rubbery. Maybe it's some kind of seaweed or coral or something from Fiji?"

"Maybe?" Samuel scowled at the thing to hide his fear. Now he would have to touch it. Greg would expect him to. Still scowling, he stretched out a finger and pressed the thing lightly. He could feel his heart pounding and sweat forming on his upper lip. He pulled another face.

"Yep. Hard on the outside." He made himself knuckle his finger and tap on the thing. "Knock, knock. Who's there?" He cocked his head as if listening. As he'd hoped Greg laughed and mimicked his gestures.

"Come out come out whoever you are?"

Samuel laughed and leapt to his feet. He snatched up a length of driftwood from the pile of smelly seaweed and debris at his feet. A cloud of midges flew into the air, and sand hoppers leapt about like fleas. Samuel didn't mind them. He brandished his stick at the thing. "Don't mess with me!" he growled in his best Darth Vader voice–a thing he'd taken weeks to perfect. He used it on the girls at school, and they ran screaming. All, that is, except that red-haired girl, Lucy. She never ran away, just stood their scowling at him, like she knew he wasn't fearsome at all.

He stalked the thing on the beach, baring his teeth and breathing like Darth Vader.

Greg was quick to find a driftwood stick and join in. "Death to the imposter!" he shouted, tossing off his hat so his dark hair flopped over his forehead.

Samuel made several sweeping slashes over the thing with his lightsaber, imagining the thing exploding into a million pieces.

"Vanquished!" he yelled, thrusting his lightsaber at the thing. His weapon buckled and broke. He fell to the sand, clutching at his throat, groaning and writhing. "It's got me!" he croaked. He writhed a few more times then went still, eyes open and staring. He could hear Greg laughing, and after a bit he sat up with a grin and picked his hat off the sand where it had fallen and put it back on his head, turning the brim to the back like before.

Greg tossed his stick away and both boys wriggled on their stomachs close to the thing and, propping their chins in their hands, fixed their gazes on it.

"Let's take it home," said Greg.

Samuel bared his teeth and gave an exaggerated sniff. "Nah. Not having that fish puke in my room." Despite his bravado of a few minutes ago, he was still cautious. "It's probably too heavy." He remembered how his lightsaber had snapped like a matchstick.

"Right." Greg scrambled to his feet. "Let's try lifting it."

Samuel got to his feet. He spat in the sand to show how tough he was and wiped his sandy hands on his jeans. "What if it's a bomb?" he said.

"It's not a bomb." Greg already had both hands on the thing and was heaving. "Get the other end," he puffed.

Samuel had no choice but to do as Greg asked. Emitting his Darth Vader hiss he bent and felt gingerly under the thing for a handhold.

"Heave!" yelled Greg.

Both boys heaved with all their might.

"It's too heavy!" Greg let it drop.

"Arrrgh!" Samuel fell back with pretended disgust. His heart was racing and his skin felt clammy. He ploughed his hands through the sand then rubbed them together, wiping away the greasy ghastly feel of the thing. "We'll have to cut it in half," he said before Greg could suggest it. It was pretty safe suggesting that because he knew they had nothing to cut it with. A stick wouldn't be much use.

Greg dropped to his knees again and frowned at the thing. "What if it's alive?"

Samuel shrugged as if he didn't care. "Tough." From the corner of his eye he could see the first of the early morning walkers coming their way along the beach. What a relief! He swallowed, but made a pretend kick at the thing just to show Greg that he wasn't finished with it yet.

Leading Naturally from One Scene to Another

This has to be done sincerely and as seamlessly as possible so that it appears a natural progression in the story.

In the final paragraph above, Samuel sees the first of the early morning walkers coming their way along the beach. This **leads naturally** into the next part of the story and introduces new characters while still staying in Samuel's POV.

Let your main protagonist have the last word.

He swallowed, but made a pretend kick at the thing just to show Greg that he wasn't finished with it yet.

The new characters are there for the purpose of moving the story forward and allow the two boys discussion about the "weird thing."

"What have you got there, boys?" A woman stopped beside them and gave them a friendly smile.
"Don't know," said Greg.
"Probably something live," said Samuel.
"Mm." The woman frowned at the thing. "Probably a lump of fat from one of the fishing boats."
Fat? Samuel nearly laughed out loud. And here he'd been scared of the thing! "Yeah, probably," he agreed. "We couldn't lift it." Fat was heavy, he remembered.
"Or it might be cheese," the woman added, squatting down beside the thing and poking at it. A piece of crust fell to the sand, and she picked it up, crumbling it between her fingers and then holding her fingers to her nose. She grimaced. "Definitely one or the other," she said firmly. She straightened up with another smile.

When more people arrive, "the plot thickens."

A small dog raced up to them, sniffed at the thing, before racing away with a sharp bark. Behind the dog strode an elderly couple.
"What's all this then?" asked the man with pretended gruffness.
Samuel sent him a grin. "We found it."
The couple frowned at the thing.
"I'm guessing it's a lump of fat off one of the fishing boats," said the first woman.
"Or cheese," said Greg.
"Stinks," said Samuel.
"Well, it certainly doesn't look like pumice or seaweed." The man bent closer.
"No." The second woman knelt down and prodded at the thing.

Her husband joined her and he too, prodded at the thing. Not satisfied with his efforts he searched round for a small rock and bashed off a chunk. They all peered at it. Under the brown crust it was a dirty creamy yellow, and smooth, with darker streaks. Like fat or cheese, thought Samuel. He was beginning to lose interest in the thing and wished they could go. He tried signalling to Greg, but Greg was gawking at the thing.

More people came along the beach, and soon a small crowd gathered. Everyone had an opinion on what the thing might be. They took photographs with their cell phones, sending them off to friends.

Someone called the local newspaper, and a man came rushing along the beach with a camera.

"We ought to call DOC," suggested Greg. "This might be something important. A new find..." Others agreed, and someone used their cell phone to call the Department of Conservation.

By the time two people from DOC arrived, it was nearly lunch time. The crowd had grown bigger and bigger as news of the strange thing on the beach had spread. A television crew turned up and began asking questions. They wanted to know who had found it and Samuel and Greg had to pose beside the thing. Samuel hated the thought of being on television, but he put on his biggest grin and tried to look "staunch."

One man said it might be ambergris, and this caused quite a stir.

"What's ambergris?" Greg asked.

"Something a whale excretes," the man from DOC explained, "after it's killed and eaten a giant squid. The ambergris is the squid's beak, and very rare. It's used in perfumes. And worth a lot of money."

At this, people rushed to get sticks and stones and anything else they could find to cut chunks off the thing. Samuel stood watching them. His guess hadn't been far out. Not fish's puke, but fish's poop. Expensive fish's poop. (Although he knew whales were mammals.)

"Let's get a bit before we miss out," said Greg.

Reluctantly, Samuel helped Greg gouge off a chunk. They dragged it to their bikes in Samuel's sweatshirt, a sweatshirt he swore he'd never wear again.

"Not likely to be ambergris," said an expert on TV that night, holding up a piece of real ambergris. Ambergris was smaller, rounder and mottled grey. Sometimes dark brown or even black.

"Typical!" thought Samuel, glad Greg had taken the piece of fat or cheese or whatever it was to his home. He hoped he'd heard the last of it.

Chapter Endings

Once again, let your main protagonist have the last word. This is Samuel's story.

"Typical!" thought Samuel, glad Greg had taken the piece of fat or cheese or whatever it was to his home. He hoped he'd heard the last of it.

By stating that Samuel hoped he'd heard the last of it, the reader knows the opposite will be the case.

And sure enough, the dreaded "weird thing" is there to torment Samuel again at the start of the new school term.

"All right, class," said Mrs Watson on the first day of the new school term, waving several clippings about the thing from different newspapers, and a blown-up colour photograph of Samuel and Greg standing beside the thing that had "starred" on YouTube. "This can be your science project for this term."

Oh, dear. Now Samuel not only has to face up to the "weird thing" and his involvement in finding it in front of his class, but it's to be his science project for the term.

But there's more. Isn't there always? Samuel is about to receive a shock!

"Sort yourselves into groups of three and work on ideas together," Mrs Watson stated. "Samuel and Greg, seeing as you two found the object, you can choose one other to join your group. But it must be a girl. I want mixed groups. Part of the project is learning to work with fellow classmates of the opposite gender."

Samuel looked round knowing the rest of the class was staring. He hated that Mrs Watson had propped the colour photograph of him and Greg on the white board where everyone could see it. He gave a shrug, as if he didn't care who joined them. As usual, Lucy was scowling. What was it with her? Something made him beckon her over. She came slowly and stood before him. She was still scowling.

Embarrassed now–the whole class had noticed, and he could sense Greg's surprise–Samuel gave another shrug. He could feel his cheeks beginning to burn.

"You can join us if you like," he said, and hissed his Darth Vader breath hoping to scare her. "But we don't want any stupid girly things, like pink handbags and…?" He searched about for something else that was girly, and shrugged again. "Whatever."

Lucy actually smiled. It was the first time she'd ever smiled at him, and Samuel felt kind of strange about it. That was, until he noticed that her mouth was smiling but her eyes weren't.

"Scared of girly things, Samuel?" she asked.

This instalment shows both Samuel's feelings about the science project and his reaction to having to work on the project with a girl. Something makes Samuel choose Lucy. He has tried to scare her away before, but she scowls at him. He throws down the gauntlet; "You can join us if you like."

But Lucy is not scared. She picks up the gauntlet.

"Scared of girly things, Samuel?" she asked.

Plot-Stacking or Layering Your Story

Now Samuel's problems deepen; how will he deal with both the science project, *and* Lucy?

Always keep adding to your protagonist's problems. This is called **plot-stacking** or **layering** your story. By adding problems for the protagonist to solve, you add depth and intrigue to your story and keep it moving forward.

The reader will be interested to see how Samuel copes with Lucy.

Humour

Use **humour** wherever you can especially if it reveals another aspect of character. In the above excerpt, Samuel gets into a muddle when he challenges Lucy.

"You can join us if you like," he said, and hissed his Darth Vader breath hoping to scare her. "But we don't want any stupid girly things, like pink handbags and…?" He searched about for something else that was girly, and shrugged again. "Whatever."

The reader sees Samuel's embarrassment and how his mind goes blank when he tries to think of something else that is girly, and only manages, "Whatever."

Show Don't Tell

Don't tell your reader that Lucy liked Samuel and wasn't a bit scared when he hissed at her trying to scare her away. **Show** Lucy not being scared of Samuel as in the above excerpt using dialogue.

Don't tell your reader that Samuel secretly respected Lucy because she was the only girl who didn't run screaming when he hissed at her. **Show** Samuel respecting Lucy through interior dialogue or the protagonist's thoughts.

As usual, Lucy was scowling. What was it with her?

Don't tell your reader that Samuel was confused in his feelings for Lucy. **Show** Samuel's confusion through interior dialogue.

It was the first time she'd ever smiled at him, and Samuel felt kind of strange about it. That was, until he noticed that her mouth was smiling but her eyes weren't.

Staying in Your Protagonist's POV

Always present the story through the eyes of your protagonist/s. Use their language, their way of speaking, thinking and behaving.

If you are in doubt of how children speak, or want to know the latest buzz words or school yard slang, visit a school with your children or grandchildren. If you don't have children or grandchildren, offer to be a stand-in parent/grandparent for a few hours. Explain your reasons to school staff. I'm sure they will offer helpful advice.

Loitering outside a school is not a good idea.

Always be honest and upfront in every aspect of your writing and research.

Chapter Fourteen

Internal Problem and Backstory

Revealing the **internal problem** is all about waiting for an appropriate time and not interrupting the flow of the story too much. Remember, less is best. Keep your explanation straightforward and to the point. Avoid adding your personal opinions of the situation; they have no part in the story.

There's plenty of time to reveal more details as the story progresses.

In the next excerpt, the children are deciding on ideas for their hypothesis and tempers are beginning to fray.

"We need to come up with something." Lucy scowled at both boys. When they said nothing, she gave a big sigh. "I suggest we each write down three ideas and vote on which one we like best."

"OK," said Greg.

"Whatever." Samuel shrugged again. At least that would mean he wouldn't have to talk to Lucy for a while. She started writing straight away. Greg chewed his pen then he, too, began writing.

Samuel sat watching them. His mind was a blank. He couldn't think of a single thing the lump of fat or cheese might have been. It was just rubbish. Waste. He wrote down waste and drew speech bubbles around it. He was busy writing waste in each of the speech bubbles when he sensed Mrs Watson walking down the aisle between the desks towards him. Quickly he squeezed the word industrial into one of the speech bubbles.

"Good, Samuel." She stopped beside his desk. "Now ask yourself the five questions 'who, what, where, when and why' and you'll have a firm hypothesis." She smiled at him.

Samuel nodded, but did not return her smile. She was being kind to him. Again. It had started during the first term, right after the "bad time" when his little brother, Michael, had died. And then his father had left. Mrs Watson and the other teachers had started being kind to him. Samuel hated it. He wanted to tell them to get out of his face. He could feel waves of sympathy coming off Mrs Watson, now, like electric currents. As if she might pat him on the shoulder or something. It made him want to rub at his arms. He nearly made his Darth Vader hiss, but stopped himself in time. He waited, holding his breath, for her to move away.

"Good idea, Marsha," he heard her say to the group behind him. His shoulders slumped in relief. Then he saw Lucy watching him. For once she wasn't scowling. Her blue eyes were misty, like she might cry or something. Gross! Now she would start with the sympathy thing. He glared at her and hissed low in his throat. She went red again and bent to her work.

Points to Note:

1. Stay in your protagonist's POV.
2. Remember, less is best.
3. Make a statement.
4. Use action and dialogue.
5. Don't overwrite or explain every detail in a huge information dump.
6. Keep to the story and don't be persuaded to venture down another pathway.
7. Avoid adding your personal opinions of the situation; they have no part in the story.
8. Don't introduce new characters here.
9. Imagine your characters as actors acting out a play on stage. (If it helps).
10. What emotion/s do you wish to portray?
11. Always stay true to your theme.

Dialogue

Use the language your protagonist/s uses.

In the next excerpt, the children are deciding what the Giant Greglusam looks like. Samuel has been elected to draw the fish.

"OK. What does the fish or creature that hatched out of the egg look like?" he asked. "It should be more fish-like, don't you think, seeing as it comes from the sea?"

Lucy pursed her lips. "Yes, definitely fish-like."

"Yeah, but more creepy and stranger than any fish we know," said Greg.

"OK. Big head with a smaller body, or small head and bigger body?" Samuel drew a couple of lines on the paper.

"Big head," Greg and Lucy said together.

They all laughed, and when Lucy and Greg leaned closer, Samuel began to feel his enthusiasm returning. He laboured over a large head, making it lumpy-shaped, like a giant snapper. Then he drew the eyes.

"Too small," said Lucy.

Samuel made them bigger.

"Yep," said Greg. "And make 'em mean looking. This is a mean fish, meaner than a sperm whale fighting a giant squid."

Lucy rolled her eyes. "Draw really long fins sticking up from its head and back."

"What kind of fins?" Samuel looked at her.

"Like wires," said Greg. "With lights at the end, like an electric eel."

"Yes, but wider at the base, and with sharp spikes," said Lucy. "Remember this fish is mean." She emphasised the word mean and shot a speaking look at Greg.

Greg snorted.

"Don't forget we have to make this thing," Samuel warned, drawing long wire-like fins that stretched to the top of the page. He made the dorsal fins wider at the base, with the three fins graduating in height and with sharp spikes at the ends.

Humour

Use **humour** and banter between your characters to bring your scenes to life. Remember theme and plot.

The children are literally and figuratively finding their feet in these first steps of their project. Samuel feels his enthusiasm returning, although he still cautions, "Don't forget we have to make this thing."

He isn't quite there yet.

Backstory

Everything pertaining to the character's past life is referred to as **backstory**.

There are many ways to reveal backstory:

1. The simple statement–as in the above excerpt.
2. The main protagonist revealing their problem through dialogue or introspection.
3. A secondary character revealing the protagonist's problem through an argument or discussion.
4. The problem being revealed in a dream sequence or vision.

It depends on what kind of story you are writing. The main point to be aware of is not to reveal everything in a huge information dump that takes the reader out of the story.

There isn't enough room in this book to show every example of where I deepened the protagonist's internal problem, and revealed more backstory, but, following is the final piece in the puzzle.

Samuel, Greg and Lucy have just presented their hypothesis to the class.

"Any more questions?" Mrs Watson asked. When no one answered, she said, "Thank you Samuel, Greg and Lucy. We look forward to seeing the finished project." Then she turned to the class. "At the end of term we'll have a show day. You can invite your parents and grandparents and caregivers to come along to view your projects. There will be a small prize for each of the top three ideas voted best by classmates. Now, who's next?"

Samuel felt his enthusiasm for their fish idea evaporate. He trudged back to his desk. His mother wouldn't come. She never went anywhere these days, not even to the supermarket. Neighbours brought them groceries. Samuel met them at the door and thanked them. He hated their pitying looks, the way they often refused to take money. He wished his mother would go to the supermarket like she'd used to. He'd offered to go himself, but that had started her crying, so he hadn't offered again.

If only his grandparents lived closer. Samuel only had one set of grandparents, his mother's parents, and they lived in Australia. They'd come over when Michael had died and Dad had gone, and they'd stayed for ages, but now they were home again. Sometimes they phoned, and Samuel talked to them, but the phone calls were getting less and less. Lately, his mother hadn't mentioned them.

Samuel liked his grandparents. They spoke in a slow rolling way, but they'd been happy to take him to the beach.

One day his grandmother went with Samuel to the beach by herself.

"Why did Dad leave?" Samuel asked after they'd walked a way along the beach without talking. He knew the answer to the question, but he still asked it. He could still hear his Dad saying, "I can't take you being scared anymore, Denise," to his mother. "Ring me when you've stopped being scared." That's when he'd left. Samuel had made sure not to meet his father's eyes as he'd walked out the door. If he had, his father would have seen how scared Samuel was, too. So he hadn't looked.

Grandma didn't answer straight away. She stopped walking, her eyes all swimmy as she looked away into the distance, as if she might find the answer to his question in the waves washing up onto the beach.

"Sometimes people do strange things under pressure," she finally said.

They both cried then, and Samuel asked, "Will Dad come home?"

Again, Grandma took a long time to answer. "Probably," she finally said.

Samuel had looked up "probably" on his thesaurus; "almost certainly," "most likely," "in all probability," "perhaps," "maybe," "possibly" he read. He hated the word "perhaps." It didn't sound right. He tried not to remember the time before when his grandparents had come when Jasmine had been born. His grandfather had gone fishing round the rocks with Samuel and his father. Michael was too little to go.

Samuel's eyes began to water at the memories. He slumped down in his chair, his gaze on his knees so no one could see his face. His mother wouldn't come. His grandparents wouldn't come. And his father wouldn't come, either.

Apart from the first paragraph, this excerpt takes the reader out of the story for a short while. The final paragraph returns the reader to the present. The story stays in the protagonist's POV throughout and introduces Samuel's final challenge; will his mother come to show day? Everything that has gone before leads to this moment; this is the beginning of the transition stage. What will Samuel do now?

Chapter Fifteen

Transition Stage

The television crew who'd interviewed Samuel and Greg when they'd first found the thing on the beach arrived to follow up their story. They asked questions and took photographs of children standing next to their prototypes.

Samuel suffered the interview with Greg and Lucy, but he kept watching the door, willing his mother to walk through it. All he saw were strangers, other kids' parents and grandparents and caregivers greeting their children and grandchildren. His hands were damp with perspiration. He kept wiping them on his shorts. When Mrs Watson called for them to be seated, his mother still hadn't arrived.

She wouldn't come.

Samuel took his chair next to Lucy. He stared so hard at the prototypes the colours ran together. The smell of paint and glue made him dizzy.

"I'm nervous," Lucy whispered beside him, which didn't make him feel any better. He tried to concentrate, but the noise of chairs scraping and people clearing their throats as they settled into their seats had his ears buzzing.

In a minute the "show" would begin.

He'd look one more time. He swivelled in his chair, searching the crowded, noisy room for his mother and Jasmine. He couldn't see them anywhere, but he kept looking and looking, even when the noise subsided, and everyone quietened. Lucy nudged him. Samuel swallowed the lump in his throat and turned to face the front, telling himself that his mother was late because Jasmine was sleeping. Samuel didn't mind that his mother might miss his presentation because Jasmine was sleeping. If only she would come.

Mrs Watson crossed the room to stand in front of the line of desks. "Welcome everyone to our science show day." She smiled at the audience who clapped politely. "Students will give their presentations and then we'll announce the winners. The students themselves have decided on the winning project." She went on to explain how Samuel and Greg had found the thing on the beach which gave rise to the idea for their science project this term; but Samuel wasn't listening. He heard chairs scrape as a few latecomers arrived and tried to make as little noise as possible. He strained to hear Jasmine's baby gurgle, but he didn't hear it. They hadn't come.

Samuel hopes with all his heart that his mother will come to show day. He even manufactures an excuse for her lateness.

Samuel swallowed the lump in his throat and turned to face the front, telling himself that his mother was late because Jasmine was sleeping. Samuel didn't mind that his mother might miss his presentation because Jasmine was sleeping. If only she would come.

Samuel's desire for his mother to witness his presentation is now superseded by his only desire; that she attends at all.
Add extra layers of tension to your story where you can, deepening both the protagonist's external and internal problem/s.
Following, is the lead up to the climax of the story.
Remember, the ending is always in two parts; the **climax** and the **resolution**.

Trying to ignore his cramping stomach, he got up with Greg and Lucy when Mrs Watson called them. He hardly heard the clapping. One or two of the students dared a whistle.
They'd decided that he'd present their original idea with the original sketch, followed by Lucy with the eggs, and Greg last with the fish.
Samuel held up his sketch, hiding behind it so he didn't have to look at the audience. His heart pounded so hard he thought he might be sick. He began, trying to stop his voice wobbling as he explained how their group had decided the thing was a deep water fish egg that would hatch into a fish as yet undiscovered by man. They'd decided to call the fish the Giant Greglusam. This brought a laugh from the audience.

"Samel," a tiny voice said, and the audience laughed again.

Samuel's heart jolted. Jasmine! It was the first time she'd said his name! He let the drawing drop and searched the audience. His mother, with Jasmine sitting on her knee, waved from a chair at the back of the room.

Samuel felt a rush of relief and pleasure. He knew his face was red, but he didn't care. His mother had come! He wouldn't let the fact that his father and grandparents hadn't come spoil his pleasure at seeing his mother and Jasmine.

Short Sentences Build Tension

Study the sentences below to see how I have used short sentences to build tension and reveal the protagonist's see-sawing emotions.

His hands were damp with perspiration.
He kept wiping them on his shorts.
She wouldn't come.
The smell of paint and glue made his dizzy.
In a minute the "show" would begin.
Lucy nudged him.
He'd look one more time.
If only she would come.
They hadn't come.
He hardly heard the clapping.
His heart pounded so hard he thought he might be sick.
They'd decided to call the fish the Giant Greglusam.
This brought a laugh from the audience.
"Samel," a tiny voice said, and the audience laughed again.
Samuel's heart jolted. Jasmine!
It was the first time she'd said his name.
Samuel felt a rush of relief and pleasure.
He knew his face was red, but he didn't care.
His mother had come!

Tone and Foregrounding

In the excerpt and sentences above, notice where the **tone** of the story changes from the high tension of Samuel willing his mother to appear and willing himself not to be scared/sick.

The sentence; They'd decided to call the fish the Giant Greglusam is where the tone changes.

The sentence reveals several things; this is a joint decision, a true team effort. Samuel, Greg and Lucy have worked together on their project and are proud of their efforts and friendship.

Samuel has managed to present his side of the project successfully. He has conquered his fear and even collected a laugh from the audience. He begins to feel better.

This is called **foregrounding**–paving the way, or setting the stage, for the next scene; time for Samuel's mother to appear.

This brought a laugh from the audience, relaxes both fictional audience and the reader, and leads naturally through the climax of the story.

"Samel," a tiny voice said, and the audience laughed again.
Samuel's heart jolted. Jasmine! It was the first time she'd said his name! He let the drawing drop and searched the audience. His mother, with Jasmine sitting on her knee, waved from a chair at the back of the room.
Samuel felt a rush of relief and pleasure. He knew his face was red, but he didn't care. His mother had come! He wouldn't let the fact that his father and grandparents hadn't come spoil his pleasure at seeing his mother and Jasmine.

Samuel receives a bonus surprise when Jasmine says his name for the first time. There will always be places in your stories to add these extra touches.

Show Don't Tell

Samuel feels relief, pride and joy that his mother has found the courage to leave the house and attend show day. Her courage gives Samuel added courage. He has braved the presentation, now he feels on top of the world. Anything is possible because he has already won the best prize of all.

The reader knows the "bad time" will now be resolved.

Show this happening. Don't state the obvious be telling your reader that Samuel had already won the best prize of all, or say that his mother had taken the first step in a long journey of recovery after a terrible tragedy. This has no place in the story.

Always allow your reader to make up their own minds about your characters and events, and to work out the obvious for themselves.

The Resolution

The resolution is where any remaining questions are answered.

Lucy was busy explaining about the eggs, but he hardly heard because he couldn't take his eyes off his mother and Jasmine. His family. He was so proud of them!

Greg held up the Giant Greglusam and flashed the fin lights. Their fish looked awesome! Everyone clapped and cheered.

Samuel raced back to his chair. He was grinning like mad.

Marsha, Christine and Troy were next with their real cheese from the moon idea. Inside the cheese, a microchip so minute as to be virtually undetectable, sent information back to outer space.

"And everyone had better watch what they say or aliens will take over the world," cautioned Marsha, drawing laughter from the audience.

They'd made a large prototype of both cheese and microchip. They got a big round of applause, as did Annabelle, Rory and Kylie with their idea, volcanic matter from the distant shores of a newly risen Pacific island.

All too soon the presentations were over and it was time to announce the winners. Mrs Watson crossed to stand at the front of the room again. She withdrew an envelope from her pocket. "The votes have been counted." She smiled and undid the envelope.

Samuel held his breath. He thought they might win…?

"In third place is…?" Someone gave a fake drum roll, and this brought a few laughs.

"'Distant Shores,' by Annabelle, Rory and Kylie." The audience clapped as the three children got up to receive their prize.

When they'd returned to their seats, and the audience had quietened once more, Samuel found he was holding his breath again.

Mrs Watson held up another envelope. "In second place…?" More fake drum rolls and laughter. "The Giant Greglusam! By Samuel, Greg and Lucy."

The audience erupted into claps and cheers and whistles.

Samuel stood up with Lucy and Greg and walked to the front of the room. Somehow he found himself holding Lucy's hand as he bowed.

"Second," she gave him a wink.

"Yes!" Samuel winked back. A wink was much better than hissing.

Mrs Watson stood tapping the envelope on her fingers as if undecided who should receive it.

Samuel looked at Greg.

"Give it to Lucy," they said together. It was only fitting. The egg had been Lucy's idea.

Still grinning, Samuel looked at his mother. She waved. Jasmine clapped her tiny baby hands. Samuel waved back. He didn't care who saw him. His chest felt tight, but he didn't care about that either. His mother had come to his presentation. It was the first time she'd gone anywhere in months. She was smiling, talking to the woman beside her, most likely telling her that Samuel was her son.

She didn't look scared. Samuel knew that after the show she'd be ringing Dad.

To tell him she wasn't scared any more.

And Dad might come home!

Samuel took a big breath–and another bow with the others to acknowledge the audience's applause. His head spun with excitement and he thought his chest might burst. He wasn't the slightest bit scared! And while he felt bad for the others that they hadn't won, he was secretly pleased they'd got second place.

Second was OK. People, families, had "second chances." Second meant "support," "agree with," "back up," "go along with," "be with." He'd looked it up on his thesaurus. Just in case.

Lucy squeezed his hand. He squeezed right back. At that moment he felt like the biggest winner ever. As soon as the presentation finished, he'd take Lucy to meet his mum and Jasmine. His family. For now. And maybe he'd ask his mother if he could invite Lucy over one Saturday afternoon. She was OK for a girl. Maybe he'd even ask her if she'd like to come exploring with him and Greg. Who knew what else might wash up on the beach.

Both Samuel's external problem the "weird thing" and his internal problem, the "bad time" are resolved.

Samuel's mother has come to show day; she is no longer scared. Neither is Samuel. He has accepted his family and is proud of them.

There is no need for a scene with Samuel's father coming home; that's a given.

Some things are best left the privacy they deserve.

The Giant Greglusam is what's known as a coming-of-age story. The hero learns something about the wider world, and himself. In other words, he comes of age.

Chapter Sixteen

Writing for Young Adults

Books for young adults, or YA as they are known in the trade, are longer than chapter books, up to fifty thousand words and more.

Below, is the first chapter of *Timeboy Book One: Gondwana* Jupiter Publishing 2013/Judy Lawn 2018

The boys reached the quarry as the first of the sun's rays struck the yellow clay.

Matt stopped, puffing hard. The summer morning was warm, yet something about the place gave him the creeps. Not a bird or animal squeaked.

"OK, D. Show me the footprint. And it'd better be worth getting up this early for." He scowled at his nine-year-old foster brother.

D sent him a fierce look and pushed past. "I know you don't believe me, Matt, but I saw it. Clear as anything." He took off, running through the bowl of the quarry, his shoes slap-slapping on the dry clay. "It's over here." He stopped, his thin shoulders heaving. "There!" He pointed to the ground, and his young voice quivered with excitement. "There it is, just as I said!"

Matt followed slowly. He didn't believe D's claim about the giant footprint. D was always making up stories. He was a pest. Matt couldn't believe he'd given up his Sunday morning sleep-in to investigate. Orange and PJ thought him crazy to even consider it.

Matt wished he hadn't told them about D's footprint. How they'd laughed! Orange had goofed around pretending to be Bigfoot pulling faces and making revolting noises. Matt remembered how he and PJ had rolled about in stitches. PJ had told practically everyone. The whole school was laughing! Now Matt felt awful, and disloyal. He shouldn't have said anything. D was so intense, so caught up in his fantasy world.

Matt hadn't wanted a kid foster brother, especially one as weird as D.

"You'd better not be making this up," he'd said to him last night.

"I'm not, Matt. I swear. You've gotta come and see it. Please!"

Matt was about to tell him to shove off, but D's pleading grey eyes stopped him. That, and the guilty feeling he should be making more of an effort with D.

"I know D's a bit strange, but he's had it hard," his mother said from that first day, nearly a year ago now. "Try and make friends with him. He's very good with animals."

If only his mother hadn't said that. Animals and Matt were a sore point. Being the only son of two farm-loving people and being less than interested in farming and animals himself led to major problems in his life.

D's arrival had only made things worse.

"Look, Matt!" D dropped to the ground and sprawled out on his stomach, propping his chin on his hands. "Check out the size of that print!"

Matt looked. He didn't know what he'd expected. A hawk's footprint? Or maybe a rabbit's paw? Or a cow's hoof print, enlarged out of proportion as the animal slid in the wet clay? The large rounded footprint made him take a step back. He blinked and looked again. The print was still there; uncanny, too big. He couldn't make it out at all.

D's face was inches from the dried mud puddle, his gaze fixed on the footprint.

Matt fought away another shiver–and the urge to pull D away. "Probably a rabbit," he said.

"It's not a rabbit." D shook his head. "Rabbit only weigh half a kilo. This animal's gotta weigh a hundred times that." D's voice rose on the "hundred." He inched closer. "Nah. Gotta be heavier than that. Way heavier."

Matt wanted to swear, but he knew D was right. D was a walking encyclopaedia when it came to animals and birds. Matt glanced around again, noting the silence of the quarry for the second time. The macrocarpa tree, blown down last winter, lay like something beheaded, its twisted roots clotted with lumps of dry clay. All down one side of the sun-silvered trunk the cattle had rubbed against it until it was worn smooth. He wanted to run his hand along the polished wood, to reconnect with the familiar.

Something moved then, off to his right. His gaze swung to catch the movement, a flash of dark grey hide, touched with strange markings.

Goose bumps crawled over his skin. Instinct told him it wasn't a cow or a bullock or even a wild pig. He knew what they looked like. Dave on the next block had just got in a few Murray Greys; but it wasn't one of those either. The hide was too grey, too tough-looking, too strange.

His gaze came back to D, still sprawled on the clay, mesmerized by the footprint, oblivious of his surroundings. Matt dragged in a breath. "Let's get out of here." The words were out before he could stop them. What was the matter with him, allowing shadows to spook him? If only he possessed some of D's affinity with animals.

"Why can't you be more like D?" Dad was always saying these days with that tone in his voice that always made Matt feel like a loser. "D's got a great way with animals."

D hadn't heard him, anyway.

"Come and look closer, Matt." A thin arm beckoned.

Matt scowled. He didn't want to look closer. That would make the footprint real. Then he'd have to think what had made it.

"Yeah. I can see it." He tried for an offhand tone. "Come on, D. It's just an old rabbit got his foot caught in a possum trap and it grew all deformed. Maybe it's even a possum, or one of the cattle. They come through here all the time."

At that, D looked up sharply. He pushed to his feet. "It isn't a rabbit or a possum, Matt." He shook his head and his tangled black curls jangled. "And it's not cattle." He glared. "Cattle have hooves, Matt," he said as if Matt were stupid. "That's a soft-footed animal." His gaze swung back to the footprint, and he heaved in a breath. "It's none of them. It's a…?" He swallowed and tried again. "I think it's a… At least I'm pretty sure it's a…?"

A crash off to one side of the quarry made them both jump. Matt looked for the grey thing. His skin turned clammy. D must have felt something, too, for his eyes widened.

The whole quarry seemed to hesitate, to hold its breath.

The noise came again, followed by a shallow rumble that rose at the end in a weird squeak. No rabbit. No possum. No sound Matt had ever heard.

He saw D's eyes widen further, but when a silly grin spread over his features, and his head started turning this way and that as he searched for the thing that had made the noise, Matt's blood ran cold.

By the time he got his act together, D was off and sprinting towards the sound.

Opening Sentences and Word Choice

I chose the strong **verb** struck in the opening sentence to help convey the harsh atmosphere I wanted, and to introduce a spike of danger and mystery. If I'd used a softer verb for the sun's rays like, touched or crept it would have painted an entirely different picture and atmosphere.

The assonance in sun's rays struck also add to the harsh atmosphere.

In my original manuscript I wrote like the blade of a knife but decided the simile was overdoing things and that I'd stick to the less is best theory. What do you think?

Verbs and Colour Words

Use strong verbs, actions words, or colour words as I like to call them: squeaked, scowled, slap-slapping, heaving, quivered, frowned, goofed around, rolled, dropped, crawled, sprawled, propped, shiver, inched, flash, touched, spook, slotted, rubbed, dragged, jangled, rumble, sprinting

Add Tension with Descriptive Words and Short Sentences

Short sentences crank up the tension in your story:

1. The first of the sun's rays struck the yellow clay.
2. The place gave him the creeps.
3. Not a bird or an animal squeaked.
4. The silence of the quarry.
5. The tree lay "like something beheaded."
6. The whole quarry seemed to hesitate, to hold its breath.
7. To reconnect with the familiar.
8. Sun-silvered trunk.
9. Pretending to be Bigfoot.
10. Weird squeak.
11. Tough-looking.
12. His skin turned clammy.
13. A thin arm beckoned.
14. "That's a soft-footed animal."
15. No rabbit. No possum. No sound Matt had ever heard.

Contrasting Characters

Each character views their surroundings through different eyes. D is enthralled by the quarry.

"There!" He pointed to the ground, and his young voice quivered with excitement. "There it is, just as I said!"
"You gotta come and see it. Please!"
"Check out the size of that print!"
He is "mesmerized" by the footprint.
A silly grin spread over his face.

Matt sees the quarry differently.

The place gave him the creeps.

He couldn't believe he'd given up his Sunday morning sleep-in to investigate the footprint.

Matt scowled. He didn't want to look closer. That would make the footprint real. Then he'd have to think what had made it.

Goose bumps crawled over his skin.

His blood ran cold.

This clash of personalities adds an extra dimension to the story–the **internal problem** for the characters to solve.

D is wonderful with animals; Matt hasn't a clue.

D is forcing Matt out of his comfort zone; Matt is only there because he knows he should be making more of an effort with D.

The **external problem** is the footprint. To whom does it belong?

Mixing Dialogue with Narrative to Keep the Story Moving Forward

In the following excerpt, the adventurers–now four as Matt's friend, Orange, his sister, Samantha and her friend, Melanie followed them–have built a platform high in a large tree away from danger; now they wait for dark.

"So where are we exactly?" Sam asked.

It was almost dark, and they lay stretched out on the platform. Noises came from everywhere; grunts and calls of animals as they foraged on the forest floor, the scream of a smaller creature as it became a larger predator's dinner, the creak and rustle of wind through trees, the river rattling over stones.

"D said Gondwanaland." Matt watched the leaves above shake and shiver as something crawled along a branch.

"I've heard of that," said Melanie. "It's when Africa, Asia, Australia and New Zealand were joined."

"Yeah, something like that." Matt squinted up at the branch. The thing had stopped moving. Was that a good or bad sign?

"So this is what the world looked like when dinosaurs reigned supreme. Weird, eh?" Orange said.

"Yeah."

"Didn't an ice-age kill off the dinosaurs?" Sam asked.

Matt nodded. "Yeah, I think so."

"Funny that an ice-age happened and we're supposed to be going through global warming," Melanie said. "Wonder when?"

"Don't know." Matt hadn't taken his gaze from the branch. The thing still hadn't moved.

"I'm starving." Orange, finished with philosophical conversation, started again on his favourite subject; food, or in their case the lack of it apart from disgusting river water.

Matt's stomach rumbled. He'd been trying to ignore how hungry he was.

"Man, I'd kill for a burger!" Orange's stomach rumbled louder than Matt's. "Triple Decker with all the trimmings. Even cucumber. And I hate cucumber."

"Stop talking about food, O," Sam groaned.

Matt's mouth filled with saliva at Orange's mention of a burger. "And fries." He pictured a large bucket of chips steaming hot and sticky with too much salt.

Orange groaned. "Yeah, three large fries. I could eat the lot in one mouthful."

After a short silence Melanie asked, "When will D and Paul be back?"

"Some time in the morning." Matt had been trying not to think about D or Paul. Or PJ. "Probably nearer midday." He remembered the desert.

"I'm gonna have me a banquet when we get back. Everything on the menu." Orange began running through the list.

Melanie and Sam both told him to be quiet.

Matt, who was trying, unsuccessfully, to tune Orange out, noted the thing on the branch above was on the move again. Another snake? He hoped not. A lizard? Small and harmless. Hopefully! A rat? Did rats live in Gondwana? Possibly. If there were cockroaches, then there had to be rats. His skin tightened at the image of both crawling on him as he slept. No way was he falling asleep! He tossed up about telling the others then thought better of it.

Orange was having too much fun listing things to eat at every fast food restaurant.

"... And two chocolate Sundays to finish off with. Then I'll start at the beginning again." He laughed, before his laugh turned into another groan. "I'm starving! We should have killed that stupid horse/deer dinosaur, Matt. Made a fire and cooked the thing. You could cook it, Matt. Mm, imagine roast beef. Probably taste the same as any other beef or perhaps venison. What do you reckon?"

"That's the second time you've said Matt could cook, O." Sam propped herself up on one elbow and glanced across at Matt. "Do you cook, Matt?"

"Sometimes." Matt made his voice offhand.

"We should have made a fire." Orange hadn't finished. "Instead of this stupid platform. A fire would frighten away dinosaurs. And give us somewhere to cook food. I'll bet there's fish in the river, trout or something. You could cook one of your dishes, Matt. Fish pie with vegetables, there's bound to be vegetables here, something edible, maybe spice or something." He licked his lips.

"Spice?" Melanie gave Matt an enquiring look.

Matt all but groaned. O and his stomach! He was spared a reply as the thing in the branches above caught his attention again. He thought he detected ears.

"Something's moving on that branch." He kept his voice matter-of-fact as he pointed, wanting to change the topic of conversation but not wanting to scare the girls.

"Where?" Both girls peered upwards.

"It's only small," Matt reassured them. "I'm going to scare it. It's a probably a dumb lizard." He sat up slowly, his gaze never leaving the branch.

"I don't see it?" Orange frowned up at the branches.

"It keeps stopping then starting up again." Now Matt couldn't see it either. He cast round for one of the sticks they'd collected. "I'll hit the branch with this." He lifted the stick and took a swipe at the tree. And missed. He sprang to his feet.

"What if it's another cockroach?" Orange was on his feet, too.

"Probably a lizard. Get ready to kick it off the platform."

"OK." Orange assumed his best imitation Kung Fu stance.

"What if it's one of those things from J Park?" Melanie shivered. "What if there are hundreds of them?"

Matt swung the stick again and struck the branch hard enough to make his arm jar. The thing landed with a small thump on the platform, scuttled across Orange's foot, and disappeared over the edge of the platform.

"Agh!" Orange kicked out blindly, tripped himself and crashed to the platform, making the construction shudder, laughing as he fell. "I got it, though."

"You missed completely, O." Sam laughed.

Matt laughed, too. He dropped the stick beside the stones. "Let's hope that's the first and last one, whatever it was."

What the Scene Reveals

Without the addition of the "lizard thing" to add tension and anchor the scene, and Matt's secret being revealed, the scene might have been flat with just the discussion about food and how hungry they are. Although, the philosophical discussion at the beginning of the section works to reveal details of Gondwanaland and their sketchy knowledge of the prehistoric world.

This is how you can seamlessly introduce both character and narrative details throughout your novel. There's no need to reveal all in the first chapter. Keep your readers guessing–and turning pages.

Now that Matt's secret has been revealed, what will the repercussions be?

The Right Moment

In a later scene with his father–after Matt and his friends return from Gondwanaland–Matt finds the courage to tell his father that he wants to cook. Until that time, his father has no idea of Matt's love of cooking.

It's all about waiting for the **right moment** in the story to deepen both your protagonist's internal and external problems.

You will know when the time is right; trust your instincts.

Chapter Seventeen

Tone/Mood

We convey **tone/mood** through our word choice, our "writer's voice." Our attitude towards our theme/s–how strongly we feel about our subject–will also affect our **tone/mood**.

The tone can be serious, sad, sarcastic, nostalgic, aggressive, jovial, or any other emotion you wish to represent.

Your choice of tone/mood might depend on your choice of genre. It doesn't naturally follow that you have to use a sombre tone for a murder mystery; a humorous and self-depreciating tone can be just as entertaining–it depends on your characters.

I've written gentle stories with soft nostalgic tones, and other stories that use a harsh or aggressive tone.

What **tone/mood** do you wish to convey?

Following is the beginning of my YA short story, *Kirsty*, published in my short story collection, *The Other Side of Solitude* Judy Lawn 2017

The morning was too hot. It was in your face heat, scooped up by the wind, heavy with the smells of the rush hour traffic, coming straight at us. Hot. The road was already starting to melt and the cars whizzing past, sprayed out stinky black tar. Yesterday had been hot, too. But today it was going to boil.

We dragged along the footpath. Colours everywhere slashed at us; bright cars, glary white buildings and the ghastly orange of a shop front door. Restless with it all, we sighed and shrugged at our backpacks and jostled for position on that hot pavement.

Kirsty swore loudly as she fought her way past an over-hanging bottle brush, its spiky leaves and fire-engine-red bracts striking her in the face.

"Bloody tree! I'm sick of banging into it!" She yanked at a branch until it tore from the tree with an angry "crack!"

Laughing, thrilled, we swung about on the footpath, darting looks all round to see who had seen…? That man in the black car, looking, then away; bus passengers, blank-faced. "For goodness' sake!" from a pedestrian hurrying past, and such stares at the length of our uniform skirts.

"Cool!" said Shelly.

"Yeah." Brie flicked back her hair and we rushed to help in the destruction of the branch. As it crunched to the pavement, stabbing out thin red needles and sharp leaves, we squealed and leapt back before it could get us.

Kirsty laughed and kicked at the broken branch. "It's only a weed."

A truck thundered past then, the driver blasting his horn at us. That nerve-jolting blare of noise in the crush of morning traffic made us jump and shriek like parrots. We fell about giggling and grabbing at each other as if we'd had the fright of our lives. Kirsty gave the truck driver the fingers and hauled at her backpack so hard her way too short uniform skirt rode up her thighs.

"Come and get it," she yelled. "Chickeeeeen!"

The truck's brake lights flashed, red and huge and we laughed and shrieked some more. When the traffic lights turned green–our saviour–the driver had to accelerate away with the rest of the stampeding herd.

"Ohhh!" went Shelly.

"I thought he was going to back up!" gasped Brie.

"Don't!" I begged, clutching my stomach.

"Chicken," said Kirsty again, but she was laughing so hard she could hardly say the word.

A car pulled up beside us at that moment with such a screech of brakes, I'm sure we all nearly wet ourselves.

"Want a lift?" Cheeky Jason McKay from our year, asked. Four other youths, in school uniform, leered out.

"And just where would we sit?" Kirsty, quite recovered, flounced across to the car.

"On our laps, Babe." The driver gunned the car.

"Tempting." Brie crossed to Kirsty's side. Shelly and I followed, drawn like magnets.

"Yeah, reeelly tempting." Shelly lolled against the thrumming car, inspecting her dark plum nail polish.

"In your dreams, dudes," I dared, stunned at the hot rush of words. Usually I left the dares to the others.

Layering, Repetition and Word Choice

Let's look at how tone/mood is established in the first paragraph by using **layering**, **repetition** and **word choice**.

The morning was too hot. It was in your face heat, scooped up by the wind, heavy with the smells of the rush hour traffic, coming straight at us. Hot. The road was already starting to melt and the cars whizzing past, sprayed out stinky black tar. Yesterday had been hot, too. But today it was going to boil.

It's all about the heat; and not languid summer sunshine desirous of lazing about in a bikini heat which would create a soft nostalgic tone/mood.

This heat is nasty, smelly, heavy, windy, glary and boiling which creates a rough, aggressive tone/mood.

Everything is moving fast; the heat, wind, rush hour traffic, cars whizzing past, the stinky black tar, a truck thundering past, etc.

Escalating Repetition and Short Sentences Crank up the Tension:

1. The morning was too hot.
2. Hot.
3. Yesterday had been hot, too.
4. But today it was going to boil.

Connotations

The road was already starting to melt, alludes to the fact that things are starting to unravel; tempers are fraying.

Today it was going to boil suggests that things have reached "boiling point." Something is going to happen, and it's not going to be pleasant–things are going to "boil over."

The scene is coated in stinky black tar which further suggests someone is going to get into deep trouble and won't be able to, or perhaps wish to, extract themselves. The "tar" and "stink" will touch all concerned.

There is also the other meaning; "tarred with the same brush." Although the girls egg each other on and rush to help Kirsty in her destruction of the tree, none are quite as daring or as badly behaved as Kirsty. Yet, because they are with Kirsty, they are seen by everyone else to be as badly behaved–the man in the black car, blank-faced bus passengers, the pedestrian hurrying past, such stares at the length of our uniforms, and the truck driver; they are "tarred with the same brush."

Always search for the right words and phrases that present the connotations, mood/tone you need for your story.

Building Atmosphere

Read through the rest of the excerpt and note the verbs, colour words and phrases which help build **tension** and **atmosphere**.

Colours slash and are glary and ghastly. Kirsty swears loudly. Spiky leaves and fire-engine-red bracts strike Kirsty in the face. She tears the branch from the tree; it makes an angry crack!

The other girls rush to help in the destruction of the branch. They leap back as it crunches to the ground. The tree stabs out thin red needles and sharp leaves.

The girls squeal and shriek like parrots. Onlookers stare and exclaim.

A truck thunders past and the driver blasts his horn. Kirsty cheeks the truck driver. The brake lights flash red and huge.

A car pulls up beside the girls with a screech of brakes. The youths leer. The driver "guns" the car. Shelly lolls against the thrumming car.

There is nothing peaceful or harmonious about the scene. It is "full of sound and fury." (Shakespeare: Macbeth Act 5 Scene 5 Page 2)

Careless, reckless Kirsty is courting trouble with a capital T. Her sidekicks try to keep up, but are no match for Kirsty as she "throws caution to the hot winds."

Secondary Characters

Allow your characters their roles in your stories, even your **secondary characters** or those who merely "stroll across the stage" and are never seen again.

Every character must exist for the purpose of moving the story forward, of revealing character through action, dialogue or introspection.

Kirsty is the leading actress; the other girls are the supporting cast.

The man in the black car, blank-faced bus passengers, the pedestrian, truck driver and the schoolboys are "bit players" and exist wholly to highlight the girls' actions, to **reveal character**.

In the following excerpt another character "strolls across the stage." What does her existence reveal?

We came to the bridal shop on the corner and pressed our faces to the window. I gazed wistfully at the white lace gowns; the frothy veils and horseshoes hung with silver and satin ribbons.

"God! Look at that," Kirsty drawled in bored tones. She blew a huge pink bubble and the pop sounded loud and disgusting and just missed sticking to the glass by a thin pink skin.

"I'm going to try it on." Brie flicked her long hair.

"You're not."

We gaped, even Kirsty.

"Yeah." Brie took a step towards the shop entrance, drawing us with her, like bridesmaids. The window spotlights followed our progress, bright confetti at our feet. This was the dare of the morning!

We had nearly reached the door when the manageress came out, carrying a broom. Sleekly groomed, in a pale blue suit, with her pale hair curved perfectly around her pale face, she looked like a ghost or someone from another planet. We stopped, stared then backed away. She didn't speak or even appear to see us. Just put her broom to the street and swept.

We staggered on, not sure if we should laugh or not.

Contrast

The manageress exists to show a contrast between schoolgirls and working girls, between youth and maturity, between refinement and crassness.

The manageress is a woman so far removed from the girls' orbit, that she might be a ghost or someone from another planet. The girls are made abruptly aware of their different stations in life: the manageress is sleekly groomed, an adult with responsibilities; they are schoolgirls, still full of childish pranks and lack of responsibility. They don't have the maturity or the confidence to speak to the manageress; she doesn't even appear to see them. They back away, confused and uncertain of how they should act.

To bring the story back to the main protagonist's POV, to allow the girls a small victory, to recover their sense of adventure and daring, I added the following:

"Another time," said Brie, daringly still within earshot of the ghost and we looked to see if she had heard. Except Kirsty, who looked bored. She gave a big sigh, but it was Brie who was queen at that moment.

"I've always wanted to try on one of those gowns." I hugged Brie's arm. What a good friend Brie was, my best friend.

"Maybe after school?" she drawled.

Oh! She was daring. Shelly took her other arm, and we went on in Kirsty's wake, slowly and sort of dreamy.

The support of her peers gives Brie the courage to issue a small challenge to the manageress. Perhaps, on her own, she wouldn't have dared. Her dare has elevated her to queen/bride of the moment–much to Kirsty's chagrin. The narrator and Shelly act as Brie's bridal attendants.

Shelly took her other arm, and we went on in Kirsty's wake, slowly and sort of dreamy.

Setting

Every setting in your story plays its part. The setting of the bridal shop the white lace gowns; the frothy veils and horseshoes hung with silver and satin ribbons presents a filmy "window to another world" for the girls; they sigh over the gowns, dreaming of their own wedding day, of a future beyond schooldays.

The window spotlights highlight their pathway to the shop entrance, enticing them towards "all that glitters."

The Character's Reactions

Initially, Kirsty resists the enchantment of the wedding gowns, feigning boredom. She tries to trash the shop but her huge pink bubble narrowly misses sticking to the window. She is a thin pink skin away from joining the other girls' admiration.

When Brie wants to try on a wedding dress, drawing us with her, like bridesmaids, even Kirsty can't resist; revealing that *all* the girls secretly believe in the "Cinderella dream."

Deepening the Protagonist's Internal Problem

Another excerpt from the story reveals something more of Kirsty: perhaps an explanation of why she behaves the way she does.

What do you think?

There will always be a place in your story where you can reveal insights into your protagonist's nature. It's all about waiting for the right moment. Remember, you can use introspection, or, as in this instance, a conversation between the two main protagonists to reveal the protagonist's internal problem.

> Kirsty's bedroom walls were bare.
>
> "Mum doesn't want any pictures on the new wallpaper," she'd explained when I'd asked. "We're trying to sell."
>
> But something told me that even if the walls had been covered in faded wallpaper, they would have been bare. The only photograph Kirsty had in her room was a small one of a handsome blond dude hugging a surfboard.
>
> "Who's this?" I'd asked once, picking up the photograph to study the blond surfie. "He's a real babe."
>
> "Don't touch that!" Kirsty snatched the photograph off me and replaced it back on her dressing table with such a tender gesture I was amazed. Kirsty

was never tender. She was reckless, careless, insolent and uncaring, but never tender.

"Who is it?" I asked again.

Kirsty flopped back on her bed, tucked her hands behind her head and stared up at the ceiling.

"Someone I knew in Tauranga."

I waited, expecting more.

"He's dead," Kirsty finally added. "You know, bought it on a bad corner. Crash, bang, that's it. Dead." And she jack-knifed into a sitting position to slam the photograph down on its face, nearly smashing the glass.

"Don't ever mention it again." She sprang from the bed to grab up her jacket. "Let's go to the mall," she flung at me.

When we'd met up with the others, later, Kirsty had been laughing and joking and insulting anyone who crossed her path, same as always.

Revealing Emotion

There must always be a reason your characters behave the way they do, otherwise they are acting out of character.

Without the above scene to show a softer side of Kirsty, to reveal that she *does* have deeper feelings, that she has suffered, she is in danger of appearing brash and blasé.

Now that the reader has a clearer insight into her character, their sympathy/empathy is aroused. Kirsty is not yet ready to talk about her experience, even to a friend. She has reacted to her loss by taking it out on everyone else, by trashing her life.

The narrator sees another side of Kirsty and shares her amazement at Kirsty's sudden tenderness with the reader.

Kirsty, furious at her lapse, reacts accordingly by slamming the photograph down on its face nearly smashing the glass.

Always allow your characters to act in character.

Show Don't Tell

Don't let your narrator offer trite and clichéd comments like, "outward appearances can often be deceptive," or "small things amuse small minds."

Clichéd comments jolt the reader out of the story by altering the tone/mood. They are irritating and (writer) intrusive. Also, they probably won't fit the character's thoughts or speech.

Always allow your readers to make up their own minds about what motivates your characters, or why they behave the way they do.

The girls are young, on the cusp of womanhood, still feeling their way into the adult world. They don't have all the answers yet. Their actions/reactions prove this.

Your characters must act in character.

Insights

You may wonder if I plan these insights at the outset. The answer is no. It's only when I examine the story afterwards that I discover these hidden elements.

It's all about choosing the right tone/mood, the one you wish to present, and sticking with it. If you begin with a soft nostalgic tone, don't change to a harsh and aggressive tone halfway through your story.

We write with instinct. Know your characters. How they behave, and why. If your characters move you, they will move your readers.

Stay true to the heart and soul of your story and you will find the right words.

Top Points to Note When Choosing Characters

1. Choose the right central character.
2. Choose a strong protagonist readers can identify with and care about.
3. What is the protagonist's problem and do they solve it satisfactorily?
4. What your characters do, how they react to the world around them, how they achieve their goals is what makes them original.
5. Your protagonist needs to be well-rounded with strengths and flaws. Make your characters real. No one is perfect.
6. All characters exist for the purpose of moving the story forward.
7. Work out your character arc–the protagonist's main problem– which will carry the story forward and not be resolved until near the end.
8. Always pose questions for your protagonists. Questions need answers. Questions and answers move the story forward.
9. Show your protagonists in action, thereby revealing their character. Don't tell your readers how your protagonists feels.
10. Always allow your characters their story, their time to shine and solve their problems however long it takes and however difficult/nonsensical those problems are.
11. Stay true to your protagonist's quest. This is their story; not a list of dramatic, overblown, unconnected events.
12. Stay true to your protagonist's chosen path. The decisions they make to solve their problems need to be the right ones for them.
13. Let the story speak for itself.

Conclusion

Writing for children is both exhilarating and challenging.

Dig deep.

Don't treat your work lightly. Children's stories deserve as much care and attention as adult stories; your story deserves your best effort.

Your efforts will reap the finest rewards; children–and adults–will thank you and love your books.

My Last Word/s

Writing is one of the great joys of my life. I love searching for new ideas, getting to know my characters, and wondering where my next story will take me.

The sky really is the limit.

If you want to write, don't let anything stop you.

Venture forth with courage and anticipation on your exciting, exhilarating writing journey!

Happy writing everyone.

Helpful Websites

Publishing

www.createspace.com

www.kindlepublishing.com

www.kobo.com

www.ingramspark.com

www.smashwords.com

www.Drafte2Digital.com

Editing

www.prowritingaid.com

www.grammargirl.com

Other Sites

www.fiver.com

About The Author

Judy Lawn has been writing for over thirty years. Her ideas for her short stories, picture books and novels come from her love of animals and nature, and a childhood spent exploring the countryside and beaches of New Zealand's North Island.

A keen fisher, Judy's first published short story was a fishing yarn, *Sam's Kingie*.

Other short stories have been published in various magazines, including New Zealand Woman's Weekly, Australian/New Zealand Woman's Day and Takahe Magazine. Two children's stories were produced on National Radio.

Her adult novels are: *Daisies Never Die* and *Watch Over Me*, the first two stories in the *Rose Rountree Mystery Series*. *Progressions* won the 2005 EPIC Award for Best Single Title/Mainstream.

Her first children's picture book was *The Shrimp Who Wanted to be Pink*, Reed Publishing (NZ) Ltd 2003. *Sebastian's Tail*, Penguin Group (NZ) was published in 2008. Two other non-fiction books on creative writing have also been published: *Creative Writing* and *Take Heart & Write*.

Judy lives on the Whangaparaoa Peninsula north of Auckland City where the many beautiful beaches and parks provide inspiration for her stories.

A long-held dream of starting her own publishing company came to fruition in 2011, with the launch of Jupiter Publishing NZ Ltd. The company ran until July 2015. Five books were published, including two children's picture books, *Jossie's New Home* and *Jamie's Monsters*.

To learn more about Judy, and to read excerpts from her novels, and the short story, *Sam's Kingie*, visit her website: **www.judylawn.com**
blog: **www.goodbounceback.com**

Bibliography

Lawn, J., and Wildman, K. *The Shrimp Who Wanted to be Pink*. New Zealand: Reed Publishing (NZ) Ltd, 2003. (out of print).

Lawn, J., and Aziz, L. *Sebastian's Tail*. New Zealand: Penguin Group, Puffin Books, 2008. (out of print).

Lawn, J., and Schollum, G. *Josssie's New Home*. New Zealand: Jupiter Publishing NZ Ltd, 2012/Judy Lawn, 2016.

Lawn J., and Schollum, G. *Jamie's Monsters*. New Zealand: Jupiter Publishing NZ Ltd, 2015.

Lawn, J., and Frongia, D. *One Haunted House*. New Zealand: Judy Lawn, 2017.

Lawn, J. *The Giant Greglusam*. New Zealand: Jupiter Publishing NZ Ltd 2014/Judy Lawn 2018

Lawn, J. *Timeboy Book One: Gondwana*. New Zealand: Jupiter Publishing NZ Ltd 2013/Judy Lawn 2017

Lawn, J. *The Other Side of Solitude*. New Zealand: Judy Lawn 2017

Printed in Great Britain
by Amazon